Caribbean Wind, Polynesian Storm

Poems and observations about
colonialism and trans history

Arvida Svenske

ISBN: 978-1-966798-62-0

Introduction

Hi! I'm Arvida Svenske, and I grew up with a sense that the world is soon coming to an end. Whether it's the climate (probably will be the climate), wars or meteors, you don't have much time and everything is in a bit of a hurry. Make the choice (what-will-you-be-when-you-grow-up?), do the thing, get chosen by the Idol jury or laughed at for losing... since the 1990's, that feeling has only accelerated and I write in frenzies partly due to this feeling. Everything has to be written down before it all ends. Because that's The End. The other feeling I've had is that history books felt like fairy-tales and vice versa. Much of it was. Our own freedom fighter/warrior king, "the uniter of Sweden" Gustav Vasa was a tyrant. The history books echoed his official 1500's propaganda by Peder Swart (his very own Goebbels) word for word. Columbus was not a swashbuckling Errol Flynn "explorer". The cops and the military are not always the good guys. I always wanted to play Native American, never cowboy, and I never wore police-suits in Cops and robbers... but we still used ongoing holocausts as fun and games in the school yard. And anything pink-dress-and-Barbie I could not even touch with my boyish hands – so I was told. It was the Spice Girls-nineties, maan. You chose sides. And all that "pink stuff" breathed fire, you could get burnt by its femininity if you happened to be born a boy, which I did. But yeah, childhood ended, and the world without veils came crashing in. Much of it was indeed ending. Sweden performed the most extreme marketization of public trains, schools, post offices and health care since Pinochet, the "strangler society" (coined by Andrev Walden) emerged – a society in which everything we own together is reduced to a minimum, and every little thing is a competition. A party started by SS-veterans, Sverigedemokraterna, got into the Swedish *riksdag*, and these are the times we live in now. Meanwhile, deep within me, something stirred – a white noise, a beach ball I forced into the waters of my innermost. This was still "a condition", a psychic illness and it was only in 2013 that the Swedish government no longer demanded forced sterilization when transgender-persons went through gender-affirming operations. Only in 2019 dared I listen to this Truth of My Heart and realize: I am a woman. Well, hear me roar. Because speaking of the end of the world, zooming out from me; several worlds have already ended. The world of the Arawaks, of the tribes of the Peruvian highlands, of the Mexican jungles, of the islands of Polynesia… they've already died. And we lost so much knowledge and lives in the process. Let's observe, mourn and reclaim that knowledge (in lieu of all the lives). This book is called *Carribean wind, Polynesian storm*. And I mean every word of it.

(Concerning words, check out the **Explain yourself!**-section for understanding. Or use Ecosia).

Arvida Juni Svenske *greets you on the other side/ of sorrow and despair/ with a love so vast and shattered/ it will reach you anywhere.*

4

Thanking...
J-FLAG, Novi Ritm (the Songs from Issyk-Kul chapter, unique for
the English version of this book, is dedicated to all the Central
Asian feminists out there), Cousins Cousines de Tahiti, all of
ILGA and all the fighting queer people, women and transgender
people – you gave me the courage and the determination.

The teachers and participants at Feminism och global rättvisa-a
course given by Färnebo folkhögskola in spring 2021, you gave me
the understanding, the lust and the determination.

All the forefathers and mothers in all the struggles, those who
wrote the words I'm borrowing.
Mum, Dad, my brother, my extended family,
friends in Stockholm, Gothenburg, Malmö
in Sweden, in the world.
To everyone at She Rises Studios, especially Katrina for
proofreading, Heather for taking me in, Hanna and Michael for all
the creative meetings, Berna and Cathrine for all the creative
input. Every person I've been in contact with has been, as they say
in Jiddisch, a mensch.
And of course, Simone (love you through all of it!) and my
colleagues and participants at Skurup och Fridhems folkhögskola in
Malmö – still love all of you.

Thank you, World,
for letting me be a part of you, I'll never take it for granted
until I probably forget it again.

Table of Contents

PART II: CARIBBEAN WIND (MINES OF GENDER DYSPHORIA) 89

PART I:

ABYA YALA- OR THE NAMES THE CONQUERORS GAVE TO YOU

India, I will call you. West Indies:
so that I can reclaim my dream.
So that nothing is lost in this
confused fantasy! It is a good picture,
and I intend to keep it.
Now get up, we will load
the heavy ships.

-Édouard Glissant

Abya Yala (deadname blues)

Whatever do you mean, America?
North, South, Central
America
Native Americans
that's not my name like Fergie
that is more the case of Cassius Clay
before becoming Mohammed Ali
and what one nation under what One God?
we never signed the finer print
nation states, capitalism?
one planet under Pachamama!

Abya Yala, speak the true name
if you mean the soil before the violence
if you mean to say in Kuna
earth in full blossom

call the dead soil America, the Big Corporation, oil-
dependency
America
speak the true name of money
blut und boden, earth and blood, a mixture
topped with blood-soaked palm-oil shaking from fracking-
trembles

say the deadname if you wish for death
say the lifename if you long for life
we all know we lost something
we are only beginning to understand
what it is

The conqueror's new name for you I

On a more personal scale
I find it a tad bit trickier
to keep up the deadname-standard
that last A is freakin' killing me
and I'm not taking away anything
I'm only adding more and more
like a super-offer plus-meny
filling up my already human brand

smash tables and demand your rights
like a crazy person all the time
or suffer internal mosquito bites
electrical gender-chocks in the gut and core

but my gender is carved in marble
social security number
like the markings on an ancient runestone
all the journals in the hospitals
the invoices and the poetry
the CV and the personal letters
I've sent them all, I've vomited
and the room is not always cleared
to step up and let your voice be heard
do heralds often proclaim
your name and specific gender?
well, what *exactly* do *you* feel like *right now*?

this is not an exam at college

but sometimes it feels like a hearing

but it's not even
Sweden's fluctuating labour market
or the taste of stale ignorance
in unenlightened break rooms burning
or the fact that I am employed
as an unpaid Wikipedia
answering intimate questions
they'd never pose to someone else
even if I'd never challenge gender
that is not what breaks the camel's back

it's my own mind playing games of chance
as I sit trying to concentrate
The Wave just comes a-crashin' in
like El Niño or the
Boxing Day-tsunami
2004,
the ones who know
they know
det stör mig när jag arbetar
I see you Nino Mick

The conqueror's new name for you II

I've spun the pale-blue globes of old
seen the names of the conquerors
thrust on places already named
how the strips of Palestinian land
has retracted like a tired tide

I've seen the lines of Sykes-Picot
the Caribbean arbitrary darts
the splitting of Hispaniola
the carving of Abya Yala

French Guiana,
Dutch East India
and all the islands taking aliases
Cook,
Wallis,
Bougainville

Greenland/Iceland
at least show creativeness
but still disdain and colonialism

I've seen the all too perfect lines
a ruler-straight split of Africa
and Asia intertwined
to a pie baked by Europe
aka the Dark Continent
it's still Tellus with its magma heart

just different *conquistadors*
most of them
bearing the pale skin
of the White Man

most of them meet mirrors much like me
of course, I'm still a conqueror
trapped inside a ruler's body

we all want to be underdogs
but most people aren't underdogs
with the same pale skin I wear for flesh

but I've stared at my incomplete
body through cold mirrors
and I think I know the ins and outs
think I know where the trouble brews

I'll wear the same silky socks
post-op too, if you know what I mean?
the same life-blues, the same kind of worries
same parents and family curses
same heart, you bet, the same liver
and so on from toe-nails to head
but when the sawdust of the flesh settles
I'll get to design my own new name
I will always give thanks to that
most did not get to do that
through the world history of victor's history
where new conquerors conquered

Cortez the killer

Cortez the fucking master killer
made a sport out of drawing blood
he hammered God's own Bolts of Miracle
into the continent he conquered
Acts of Conquistadors by guide of Higher Powers
in the name of the New world they created
Nueva España, well why not
one of the coming Empires
in which the sun never sets

the storms of woe let loose
by the European colonialism
staged
and are still staging
the greatest mass extinction
of human beings
we have ever seen

Cortez the fucking master killer
World Cup winner of Colonialism
punched God's own Miracle Needles
into the body of earth itself

it's in every single one of us

Sveaskog – they're lying
(the Scorpion and the Frog)

Many young people strangely boast of being "motivated"; they re-request apprenticeships and permanent training. It's up to them to discover what they're being made to serve, just as their elders discovered, not without difficulty, the telos of the disciplines. The coils of a serpent are even more complex that the burrows of a molehill.

— Gilles Deleuze

Sveaskog – they're lying
it's a natural thing they do
a neon-sign dwarfing Sápmi
their evil shines on through

Bientije and Lill-Skarja
Gihmiesgielas, Guossavare
Biellovare and the rest of them
they're coming so beware

baby

acolytes and apprentices
with technological fervor claims
that we will fix the oceans
forests, rivers, floods and plains

by some Eldorado-tech-machinery

yet to be found in some old glade
that is climate denial, y'all
if you see them, give them shade

Sveaskog is lying
much like Exxon, much like Shell
devil-demons, sent from Hell
human rights of the indigenous
not much value
doesn't
sell

Permafrost in Polynesia
(the voice of the White Man)

what strange set of
garments you wear
give us a few please
we can see you got spares

it's not like you've travelled
the world like we have
we've got the tools now
to carve more gold from that calf

why, does not your god
lecture and tell
on how Earth is sacred
and precious and well

well, then you can dwell there
in your reserve
and receive all the rations
that you justly deserve

and you can keep on
being peaceful and meek
the pearls for Manhattan
what do you mean, "cheap"?

I was not thinking
that you thought like that
in yields, gains and margins
and earnings and scraps

you don't happen to be
some materialist?
who wants to raise profits
like some capitalist?

well, then, you can keep it
your nature, your plants
talk to your spirits
and eagles and ants

and unto Caesar
(say… silver and gold?)
we will free you from it
you keep the mold

we were thinking you could work
in these heavy trades
huh, get close to nature
get pumped, rocking braids?

nothing's for free, sure
even heather and rags
if you didn't want us here
you should have made flags!

we would have known then
that this country was yours
we did the right thing here
see, *you* were off course

if you want to file your
little complaint

we've got a courthouse
for sinners and saints

you're all very welcome
to bring evidence
because we want to listen!
just try to make sense!

because I say unto you
your dress code, your talk
if they are so weird…
well, it's bound to be mocked

we've got our culture
it's democracy
it's been workin' since Jesus
how do you plead?

well, sure sounds lovely
leave it all to the kids
but a kid has no impulse
what if we did?

nah, y'all better figure
that little thing out
come speak the right language
let it stream from your mouth

just don't come running
with the blood and the guilt
because we want to listen
if you just wind down and chill!

A need (for deep harbors)

Calm lake wields a deep bottom
sometimes I feel bottomless
a vast woodland lake that extends ethereally
down to the magma layers and the core of Earth
my root system flares up; burn-beaten

Like the *Skogsrå* when I'm being tested
in the knowledges of femaleism
my make-up game is getting better
but my back:
my back's a hollow stem

a need for even deeper harbors
roots and acts of peculiar balances
so that the pendulum doesn't lose its pace
stands swaying like a buck-wild compass

but the natural harbors, the deep-water ports
other entities have locked them down
cashed in their
fishing rights for dim lit safety
a surprising amount of people
wants to speak against my rights as woman
meanwhile I'm in frozen limbo
no date is set for lukewarm spring
the harbor has to be cleared of ice
my application still pending

but enough about my little secret
my storm-in-a-teacup-life
I want us to meditate
Guadalope and Saint Barth
the island that Sweden bartered
exchanged for fishing rights in Gothenburg

("what do you give someone
who already has it all?"
maybe a little island
nestled in a made-up world
belonging
in the Caribbean)

you know, when bullies were rude to you
deep down in brainwash primary school
the adults would say "they're just jealous"
unsure of your security

oh, how the jealousy
most have haunted the European
when their white blind eyes saw Africa
Asia, the "Americas"
plus, all of Polynesia
and the hard-won Caribbean islands
they just struck that bully-nerve
so that the saddest people known to man
the complacent white two-legged pigs
could eat pineapples and oranges
melt sugar and toast in coffee

brew tea and discuss their nonsense
devouring and conquering
with lips of true predators

the need for a deeper harbor
my bottom is not always yours
but some of them run deeper still
and others we fill with garbage
crude anchors crush the coral reefs

and there were no limits
no ends to the deep fathoms
South Pacific girls were made to have
Caribbean women forced to put out
to stand against the tidal waves
of the lusts of European sailors
all the desire, all the violence

colonialism is the biggest crime
still being carried out

Voodoo on Ile-a-vache

You can't blame the youths
you can't fool the youths

- Peter Tosh

Napoleons men got spanked by them Haitians
Wyclef Jean raps these lines proudly
and that is the proper tone
for Haitians stood up to France
but at costs too great to ever carry

Haiti is a place of honor
of the dead who fell for war and famine

years and years and years of war
against all of the counterparts
(a small percent of an island, this)
then, when they emerged
out of the smoke victorious
against a host of overlords
and forcefully gained independence
they were forced to pay indemnities
paying it off all the way from
1820
until
1947
they paid if off, next obstacle:
American full-scale invasion

fencing off this little nation
east toward the Dominican Republic

Haiti honors those who died

Where Pirate Morgan (yes, like the whiskey) dwelled, his
killing bay
that's where the citizens of Île à Vache
still dances in voodoo-ceremonies
6000 years in the making

Haiti honors those who died

and away on Haiti proper
160,000 people died
in the earthquake of 2010
laying waste to Port-au-Prince
whole building blocks put down to dust
unblinking hopelessness
in the eyes of oh so many children

the artist collective
slash township slash quiet oasis
Artist Rezistans Haiti
working with the material
that happened to be overflowing:
skulls of people now removed
from life through the Earth's trembling

but restored and given life anew

in arts and crafts and shrines in worship
Haiti honors those who died

and the organization SAKALA
working for the orphaned children
has a Wall of Dreams where they put up
children's dreams kind of like
Philippe doctor 2028
Etienne lawyer 2030

Haiti honors those who live

The proud free island nation rising
one of the early and many victims
of the smugness of European
purring evil in the world at large

I the killing bay of pirate Morgan
Île à Vache sees a dancing crowd
Far away from the whisky brand
6000 years in the making
you cannot forbid something
older than languages and nation states

Haiti honors those who live

them bones are gonna rise again

Antillergulden

We will put our flag right here
here's some paper, some alloyed metal
showcasing kings, you will never see
depicting faces from across the sea
the ocean that we have crossed
and only we know how to make
you will never know its secret ways
but consider it your new God

national anthem? sure, go ahead
you get the first verse in your mother tongue
but the rest of the fucking song
better bleat them in Dutch, you guys
God's own chosen angel-speech
Why? Well, we say so, right?
And we've got monopoly on monopolies

Blood and sugar

The two stories of the Caribbean:
the tale of rich European
plantation owners and the other one
selling Africans by the pound
both of them are intertwined

there is Architecture and blood
there is pride and something genuine
sad places like Guantánamo
light songs like Guantanamera
but it is way too easy to give thanks and praise
to American imperialism
compare it to Fidel Castro
and the shadows he cast
a sort of inverted twisted
Soviet/Yugo-nostalgia
back to some mafia-led dictatorship
the great old bastard Fulgencio Batista
20.000 dead in seven years
by his hand and his compadres
landing softly in Portugal
under the wings of Salazar
then some business deals in fascist Spain
before his heart collapsed on him

you don't get this from Joanna Lumley's
lovely sunny documentary
armed with charms and smiles she goes to Matanzas

gets to see the Town of Poetry
the Martí-statue and the Bridge City
the golden hand that would knock the doors
of Matanzas oldest pharmacy
the lines would wind around the block
Monday nights while something brewed
hot in the heart of Cuba
from the sugar plantation barons
through the multicorporative profits
stirred a strange satellite
that became the rare radical
little rebel in the Greater Antilles
we are the wolves we feed, indeed

Mission civilisatrice

The objectively most brutal
barbarians in history
who raped, pillaged, plundered
with a heat-seeking missile's
precision and conscience
on a scale of seven continents
in a shard of the universe
they believe throughout the centuries
and the notion hasn't left them still
that they constitute the World's center
though they hold the smallest continent

and they
called it White Man's Burden
they called it
civilizing mission
they moaned it was a heavy load
they dared call it a Higher Calling

they lose, but they don't really lose
because of Commonwealth and *France d 'outre-mer*
they make money from war damages
they make money from phlebotomizing
the earth itself, cutting open veins
then they beat their white Tarzan-chests
proclaim themselves the world's white knight
and themselves the High Kings of All

and I just can't stand it anymore

Cotton cradles

The Peruvian coasts that carried loads
the fields of greed in Uzbekistan
that sucked the Aral Sea from Mother Earth
for an empty ideology
a planned economy pumped up from inside
and on the far side of the Iron Curtain
the towering Great Plains and coasts
that half of the United States
fought to keep slavery in
it's all that, and the Egyptian Nile
that forms and shapes

(the same forces that wouldn't) de-colonize Sápmi and Abya
Yala
(the same forces that wouldn't) let The Growth decrease
even a little
(the same forces that wouldn't) let Las Mariposas fly
let the hermanas Mirabal survive
(the same forces that would) divide and conquer Hispaniola
keep Austria-Hungary alive and kicking
the Ottoman Empire alive and kicking
the British Empire alive and kicking
create a Thousand Year Third Realm
keep the guillotine swinging
build a great Anti-Fascist Wall
Make America Great Again
the same cultural cradle
the same Greco-Roman heritage

with its sexual moralism
the division between Nature and Culture
the gender incongruity
the wrong turns on the roads of life

the same storm, but not the same vessels
different rudders and technologies
we all see the Pleiades shining through
we all have the ability
to face the clear gaze of the Polar Star
but we all have different
compasses and star-gazers
culture capitals,
economic interests,
the same forces within us all
who can't do it, won't do it, daren't do it

How do Men know what rivers want?
we are not on their Zoom-meetings
the river would forever flow
even without our hydroelectric plants
taking up their watered bodies to
maybe mass-spray our almond fields
stateside, California
the Peruvian, Egyptian cotton
Amu Darja is not to blame
Syr Darja is not to blame
for turning Karakalpakstan
to a salt-laden inland desert
a few years before my Dad was born

it used to be a coastal land
beside of one of the biggest lakes
now corpses of rusted engines
rots in a lonely desert
because Sharof Rashidov lied
throughout the dark decades
steady catapulting up his numbers
Moscow applauding all the while
giving him more and more profit
just like globalistic capitalism
just like private owned healthcare companies
profit-making kindergartens
profit-making elder-cares
but in a much much bigger scale
from the Caribbean
to the South Pacific

but now, a little tide is turning
the boats in the cotton cradles
rocks from rivers suing us
Whanganui can sue you, alright
Muteshekau-shipu possess the power
Yamuna can sue your ass
and Ganges can do the same
Atrato can file complaints
Vilcabamba can make demands
the dream is over
what can I say
except *I'll see your ass in court* I guess

Subcontractor blues

Woke up this morning
a storm of critic wailed like a gale
did my morning exercise
you just inhale then you exhale
something about a scandal
mistreatment on a Grand Ol' Opry-scale

Woke up this morning
a CEO of this shit
but I haven't risen to dizzy heights
by not showing some grit
well, the Devil's working for someone
but that is the subcontractor's bit

I can't 20/20
hindsight all of the way
I can call my man in Brussels
and even my man in Botany Bay
but I just don't have the number
to the man in charge in Meanchey

I've got the blues most chillin'
how I am the villain
for the wheelins' and dealins'
for the workers who's trillin'
for how the overseers be drillin'
coalitioni'n the willin'
no width to the ceiling

and no penicillin'
for the sick and the needy
see, y'all dissing the feeling
of the dizzy heights reeling
it's a jealous mischievous
plot against me, it's killin'
me, this subcontractor's blues
we will launch
an enquiry

Idamelys v patriarchy

Machismo is everywhere
a Jamaican man said to me
it was nearly ten years ago
and I haven't forgotten that
he spoke of the Caribbean
at the region at large that time
that includes Abya Yala, Khéya Wíta
unfortunately
still rings true like fire

but I saw this documentary
about Idamelys Moreno
she wants to represent Cuba
in boxing, but they will not let her
because – spoiler alert! – she's female

(we are stuck in the past
that is Cuba's greatest problem:
quote from that documentary)

in Cuba, women can't box
because– I assume–
women are supposed to mother (verb)
and not fight any freedom fights

(and I must add to all of this
that is a fact all over Earth
with quite a few exceptions though)

but unto Idamelys I say
to all fighting women, too
girls, put on those boxing gloves
step up into the boxing ring
we have a few rounds to go
against machismo, looming everywhere
until we don't have to anymore

Idamelys, let your fists fly hard
beat down that machismo-ideal
como una mariposa, una abeja
strike at them with the Iron Fists of Women
throw rocks at that machismo-shrine

you've got a lot of allies, too
transmen and transwomen
men and non-binaries
and gender-non-conformatives
melt down that machismo-ice

Now, let's talk some Estados Unidos

June gloom

June Gloom is a California term for a weather pattern that results in cloudy, overcast skies with cool temperatures during the late spring and early summer. While it is most common in the month of June, it can occur in surrounding months, giving rise to other colloquialisms, such as "Graypril," "May Gray," "No-Sky July," and "Fogust." Low-altitude stratus clouds form over the cool water of the California Current, and spread overnight into the coastal regions of California.

The overcast skies often are accompanied by fog and drizzle, though usually not rain. June Gloom usually clears up between mid-morning and early afternoon, depending on the strength of the marine layer and the distance of the location from the Pacific Ocean, and gives way to sunny skies. May and June together are usually the cloudiest months in coastal California. June Gloom is stronger in years associated with a La Niña, and weaker or nonexistent in years with an El Niño. This weather pattern is relatively rare, and occurs only in a few other parts of the world where climates and conditions are similar.

–Wikipedia, June Gloom, collected 25/9 2023

Los Angeles gives one the feeling of the future more strongly than any city I know of. A bad future, too, like something out of Fritz Lang's feeble imagination.

–Henry Miller

Fall is my favorite season in Los Angeles, watching the birds change color and fall from the trees.

–David Letterman

Los Angeles has no seasons, so it's kind of hard to keep track of time here. The lines between spring, summer, fall, and winter all blur like my vision. I get stuck on repeat for different measures of eternity.

–Kris Kudd

I wish I could put my fist through this whole lousy beautiful town.

–Rose in The Last Jedi

June gloom, Los Angelians named the weather
we came rolling in a rental car
from LAX and our relationship's
flaming crescendo, my and my ex that summer
it wasn't really a Disney-dream we had
playing our Princess-, Prince-role respectively
but fate choose Californ-a-yay
to be the sketchbook for our memories

Det är som om allt jag sagt och gjort
Samlas i Los Angeles
Till tiden då vi var där
Mitt uppe i kärleksstress

Sen är det som att iakttas
Av någon högre makt
De släcker sakta skissborden
Känslan förbleknar snabbt

No logic emerges from that General Motors-town
with its downtown-skyscraping-business
hyper-gyms, malls and gas stations
unless you have a car, car, car

how do you propose you make it to
Griffith Park with its hills and crevices
so your tourist eyes can see the Hollywood-sign
unless you go there by motorized vehicle…
can you explain yourself, *grabbatös*?

doppelgängers in LA by foot
I see the two 21-year olds
relics wandering belittled
looking like fools on the long, broad streets

but it wasn't our very own *junidimma*
our *puppy love* was a candle light
in the bleeding sun
that is
the dying California

Det sägs att hjärnans vänstra del
Håller den högra i ett schack
Och den högra, den hålls vaken

Genom varje drömlös natt

En kväll kom månljus in till mig
Gardinen hade hål
Det sa "det som varit är förbi
och snart är vintern vår"

To bypass and get off LA Freeway
was a Guy Clarke one-way-ticket out
Get-out-of-jail-free-card from Babylon
and Carmel-by-the-sea
cobbled and cuddly, *nouveau riche*-dreamy
shabby chic felt like living in The Sims
I've always liked that game, actually
my favorite past-time when I was thirteen

in the hostel and the restaurants
on the Carmel nights where we could breathe
in two days, greedily devoured
half our twelve-day-travel-budget
our relationship breathed in life anew
and in San Francisco
passing the lawns and parks
Haight-Ashbury with all the heroin hobos
and wrapped in Fisherman's Wharf-tourism
it contracted COPD and coughed
dying slowly as we took the pictures

Det kanske är övertänk
Det är säkert övertänk

Kanske är det övertänk

You could write libraries about Tinsel Town
but at the same time, there's not much to say about
El Pueblo de Nuestra Señora la Reina de los Ángeles del Río
Porciúncula
The Town of Our Lady the Queen of the Angels of the River
Porciúncula
in a way it is a paradise
the palms and Santa Monica
the greatness of the Pacific Ocean
and a childhood dream came true one day
in the car stereo as Dr Dre
rapped about Crenshaw Boulevard
the street sign saying… Crenshaw Boulevard!

and there were flickers of tiny lights
cute little Farmer's markets
cool little hipster stores
one named the Never Open Store
which, well, was never open
a great analogue clock on the house facade
just asserting this "never open"

I thought
for a minute there
I saw the soul
of Los Angeles

Och ja, det kanske är övertänk

Det är säkert övertänk
Det kan vara övertänk

Universal studios
the crowning moment of the whole darn trip
the one defining event
defining the difference between the big US of A
and Sweden better than even I as a poet could
the show ending the adventure tour
extrovert on stage so sunshiny
you got scorched and burned, needing aloe vera
telling you the *success story*
asking whether anyone
in the audience wanted to come on stage
"become a moviestar", with no exceptions
except two shy Swedish tourists
eagerly hoping they'd get picked
with the enthusiasm of the maddened crowd
at Goebbels speech in Sportpalast

poetic license, I exaggerate
but you can't over-appreciate
how much American commercialism
destroys the climate of this planet
clad in strange Disney-smiles
everyone wanting to make it big

our LA, our relationship, our peak
a scented candle in a nuclear reactor
and our memories remain to keep

something puppy-love-esque and bittersweet
the Potemkin coulisse LA
always remaining (to me) an altar
to Molok, to Baal and Mammon
it's Babylon, and not just Babylon
white rastas call the boys in blue
when they are robbed of their precious ganja
I am not joking,
(Why so serious?)
Drought sucks grass
Yellow wither-wilt
Fresh water levels die

Evian in every fridge
The US Army helicopters
Water Bombing Beverly Hills

A wounded, smoking California
Water-reserves over Harmony
Agent Orange over Tan Son Nhut

But you can't have one more Katrina
BP's "we care about the small people"

And the almonds drink like greedy camels
Our friends on the silver-screen
Need their pretty faces to stay hydrated

*So the geniuses at Turfmedix *insert brand name here**
To keep the silent status quo

Paint the grass green
Pay per square meter

The bees dying beneath the MAGA-sound
Of corporate America

these are days of Sodom, Rome, Gomorrah
orgies in the streets are up
cue the forest fires of our time
the last drops of water condensating
on the lawns of rich people
while we crouch in our sleepwalker-haze
like stars living in mud, scrolling celebrity-news
every meal like a medieval king
obsessed by entertainment systems

The day they shot Trump

A guy down at Pressbyrån
African-American, looking at his phone
on that fateful day 2016
when winter slyly ambushed Stockholm
fierce snow, we bought our morning coffee
We collectively shook our heads
First thing this gentlemen says
"He's gonna get himself shot, you know"

Things are not black and white,
rather the sombre gray
of parliamentary buildings worn by time
you can pierce ears with bad intent
donate the equivalent
of 1700 Russian rubles
to the political opponent
of the GOP you're a registered
member of and be a white, straight male

Snakes come out in the sunshine
Slugs get out in the rain

Snails literally carry their homes
On their backs and can look slimy
To look at, and to touch and feel
But only a snake has poisonous
Teeth and glands to kill large mammals

And even a presidential plan
weak and squirmy, Green New Deal-wannabe

isn't the fucking coup d'etat called Project 2025

It was a strange day, I'd been to a funeral
was in a weird place, sat with my girlfriend
Down by the lake, we talked vacation plans
And about how it felt to be alive

Spain won the European
Cup of Football, beating a bloated England
Confidence like a horny rooster
Yelling *it's coming home* , then firing
A trainer that has earned them two consecutive
silver medals, the best they've been in years

We never thank each other enough, do we?

Snakes come out in the sunshine
Snails carry homes upon their backs
A person that repeatedly
receives whip-lashes as punishments
throughout their lives by pale-skin masters
will react with hardened skin
it'll echo through ancestral DNA's

The day they shot Donald J.
Strange feelings down by Söderbysjön
It did not begin there
But it certainly set things in motions
And made it clear as silver glass
That something was wrong in America

Something is wrong in America.

Mix it up (like a Loganberry)

(At the Drag Time Story Hour)

Come, gather round, little firefighters
A story I will tell thee
About James Harvey Logan
Father of the Loganberry

A judge slash amateur botanist
(And you know amateur means love)
Made it into the Superior Court
But also, springing from his glove

A berry loved in the UK
As a Sherry trifle condiment
West New York up to Ontario
Batavia, down the continent

Mixing the European raspberry
(Rubus idaeus, the sis')
With the North American blackberry
(Rubus Ursinus, that is)

Accidental berry-breeding
Moving beyond cis
Not bad for a Santa Cruz-mistake
Breeding and creating this:

You, see, the raspberry, a *octoploid*
Aughinbaugh its pretty name
met the Red Antwerp *diploid*

Mixing the female and the male

Out of the green bush floats
the Loganberry hexaploid
If you look at it a certain way
A trans-berry was deployed

And the Logan bred the Tayberry
Youngberries, Boysens, dewberries,
Olallieberry, Marionberry
I read up on them and grew weary

But back to the mixing up
Since that is the poem's name
I only have one metaphor left:
You go girl, be the grain

Every single body
Got a mind and soul to carry
In the end we'll all get brownish eyes
Mix it up like a Loganberry

Every single electorate
Got a Red and Blue to carry (throw in socialism –
democratic!)
You already know where I'm going
Mix it up like a Loganberry

Don't change into what you're not
But wreathe a big bowl to carry
So that it can bear all the varies
Mixed up like som Loganberries

Songs from Issyk Kul (written before a cancelled trip to Kyrgyzstan)

I. Hymn of a housewife

I'm not a simple woman
But I do not ask for much

Tolrunbek, son, boil some water for me

You've asked what I find glory in
you ask what is my crutch

Tolrunbek, son, boil some water for me

All the lonely silent prayers
I've whispered to the womb

Tolrunbek, son, boil some water for me

I begged my blood for promised oaths
so that only boys would brood

Tolrunbek, son, boil some water for me

I gave three happy boys a life
they could not start before

Tolrunbek, son, boil some water for me

I never knew such sweet duress
or what I bargained for

Tolrunbek, son, boil some water for me

And to answer all your questions
about how I spend my time

Tolrunbek, son, boil some water for me

I live a life that I would say
is not entirely mine

Tolrunbek, son, boil some water for me

But as the sun sets on our village
and I look upon their smiles

Tolrunbek, son, boil some water for me

It might just be well enough
to know that I'm alive

II. Elope

to run away in secrecy
to get married to the one you love
as illustrated in The Graduate
if you freeze in on the final frame
the camera casts its zoom at them
giggling on a Greyhound bus
when the laughter fades away
you see they start to realize
"well, where do we go from here?"

there aren't enough masses of
water in the Issyk-Kul
Songköl or the Toktogul
mountains north of Karakol
walnut trees in Arslanbob
to conceal or hide or console lovers
eloping from their families
in some Tjingiz Ajtmatov
style that they've been dreaming of

because when you take that giant step
you pack your bags, you board a plane
a bus or train or automobile
the wry question wipes away your smile

because where do you go from there?

III. Jamilia did the right thing

Jamilia did the right thing
a Jeanne D'arc-beacon lit aflame
one needs love to live
and she and Daniar lived
and loved
like
crippled outcasts
of some olden tribe
injured wolves or elderly elephants
crushed by the norms of the society

Jamilia did the right thing
but was crucified for being so
much of a human being
despite being born a slave
she did not attain perfection either
like in that song by Jethro Tull
better lick your fingers clean
from the sweets of Eden you have eaten
or serpents will get to you

Jamilia did the right thing
and she did it for herself
as we're taught in our tiny Europe
to never have no bonds to others
so, do we stand alone in love?
just right after a wedding bleakens
Jamilia did the right thing
but loneliness was the price

IV. Song from Issyk-Kul

*This song is like being in a warm blanket in your childhood's
home,
with the rain pouring outside,
and everybody's doing their things except you,
just feeling the moment...
You feel safe, you feel loved.
It's a "You're going to be okay"song.*

-Amine Anli

Ice sculptures towering
over Issyk-Kul, icicles
glistening and glimmering
with a cold homely glow
hollow bones form the tune
of some kind of

love

Mountainous lake, body of Kyrgyz water
mighty pool, grant me your innermost
strength and silent dignity
and grant me some kind of

love

Stars above and I remember
another time and walk of my long life

when I gazed up there in India
a girl beside me, pointing out
an entity in the starry outskirts
said to me you're like that star
one does not see you at a first glance
but you shine brightest of all of them

Mountain body, lake of Kyrgyz water
speak to me through icicles
send the shimmering, the glistening
in tiny little shakes
of love

V. Listen to the glistening

Listen to the glistening
it's bickering, belligerence
the snickering, the twittering
the ignorance, the whispering
the silence of indifference
tells me everything'll be different
throw a couple more digits in
let the years pile on, go living, split!
there will be quiet deliverance

I stood listening to Issyk-Kul
it was telling me the this-just-in
of the world and of the bliss within
I stood small but not belittled then
caught grief from my bitch within
but came to peace with my differences
and I've felt much richer since
now, I've never had no christening
but that felt like something similar

Listen to the glistening
the peace, the silent icicles
the lake's blue-eyes tells no bit of sin
only project what you put into it

Listen to the dissidents
of Turkmenistan, Uzbekistan
Kazakhstan, even Kyrgyzstan
Tajikistan, Afghanistan
Putin's Russia, Turkey of Erdogan

in Rojava, and in Syria
Iran and China of Xi Jinping
listen to imprisoned friends
of the belittled women, belittled men
as sure as the mountains still will stand
light shall seep into the prisons and
free them from their imprisonment

Listen to the glistening
it's speaking but we are not listening
the pinnacle of civil ignorance
believe we livin' large in cities when
we sold away ourselves as citizens
giving power to the businessmen
politicians and machineries
it's a pity and we live in it
risking our own and our children's health
our humanity indifferent
nothing will stop our will to live
but we should do it in togetherness

Listen to the glistening
you might hear it in the whispering wind
in the mountains and the little springs
brooks and rivers and the little things
telling you of your strength within
rock solid yet with brittleness
we are stardust, we are kids at spring
running through meadows, a little giggle ring
life's meaning – among other things

(this is just my opinion then)

VI. In the Uzbek quarters

the sounds of the *mahalla*
dies down as Stillness rises
and war on a deathly sickness
and Kyrgyz chaos melts away

like some gust of wind before some storm
the first breath outside a respirator
the first joyous words shouted out
the village clothes itself in wedding

and the faint sound of the congregation
starts to reach through the vicinities
women's voices form a straightforward
terminal and reverential song

the girl is crying
she has become a guest
she is gently leaving us
the father's weeping for his loss
in the place of his only daughter
he will plant an almond tree

and the words from the Uzbek quarters
clothes blues in another dress
a warmth clutching for its firmament
rising slowly from the heat of Earth

blue canopies adumbrate the scenery

blue as all eternity
bride-groom simplicity
life as clear as morning sun

VII. I know my grandma's grandmother

It is a great honor and tradition in Kyrgyzstan to know your patrilineal heritage. The custom does not extend to the matrilinear side of the family. In a protest on the 8th of March in Bishkek, before covid and before the government shut it down, one of the signs said "I know my grandma's grandmother" protesting this.

she was a real-life martyr
in the plains of our ancestors
she lived and died in dry deserts
in a time where
there were no aggressive
Kyrgyz nationalist parties
aiming for the Jogorku Kenesh
trying to force a proverbial president
to wear his ak-kalpak and be a good boy

I know my grandma's grandmother
and she would not think much of it
not much of it at all
if there were, say gay clubs in the town of Bishkek

(which of course I don't imply at all
as we all know there are no gay-people
in our great and proud strong Kyrgyz land)

well, I know my grandma's grandmother
and she said she would not mind at all

I know my grandma's grandmother
she lived a full life you know
even though there were no cellular phones
no Netflixes or MTV's
to preach Americanism in

and I know for sure my grandmother's
grandmother's
grandmother
she would not budge an inch for you
no matter
how much intimidation
you'd put upon her head
I know her
and you
you wouldn't outlast her
with your decrepit masculinity
built on eagle-men and *alu kachuu*
she'd whoop your naked ass for it

so Kyrgyz nationalist parties
aiming for the Jogorku Kenesh
trying to force this on a proverbial president
wear your ak-kalpak and be a quiet good boy!

Poem of Russia (as Russia falls)

Slow horses slurps up mud
running ever brown and fat
they are stuck in excrement and lies
dragging me down into their drowsy, contented world
sour and swollen with sleep
the sky is a frail duck-board span
and upon it, month number Seven runs
little bird, Gamajon, give me hope
grant me light

-Vysotskij, in Fria Proteaterns Swedish translation of
"Kupolen" (The Dome)

'Twas a feverish, young, velvet-late Summer's Day
I had no skin against the World of it
Autumn coming on, like a tuned transistor-radio
sweeping across the Dome above
7,5 credits at a university course
strolling across SU's campus
saw my freakin' ex
everywhere

and I fell into the Slavic department
double-hour of Russian history
staggering out in the heat a drunkard
head brimming with false Ivans
tsars and steppes, barge pullers down at the Volga
and I could not perform a single action

except put on earphones and sit right down
let the Device play *Kupolen* loud

when Carsten Palmær writes the lyrics
Stefan Ringbom brings out his desperate singing voice
well, then you listen carefully
because you know they have things to say

med guld har vi ryssar klätt kupolen
så vår herre ska se på oss ofta

(We, the Russians, have clad the Dome in gold
So our Lord will look upon us often)

I saw with eyes of Youth and Death
the autumn sky and thought I'd found
the wisdom, folly, bits and pieces
glistenings of the Russian soul

like a *blitzkrieg* when the blow was struck
February 24th, 2022
a meaninglessness of a war aggression
offensive blow from a very Tsarist man
flexing muscles as in *Pumping Iron*
he wants to beat a certain gentleman
one *Iosif Vissarionovitj Dzjugasjvili*
in the game of most dumbest fucking shit

you can't beat Stalin
at his own game, self-taught master

Crazy Iosif was the absolute GOAT!
of the divide and conquer-guerilla
warfare of salami-tactics
The insanity of a perfectionist
mastering, *becoming* Soviet thought
he had read
all the manuals
already thought out
all the thoughts to think

I never knew Stalin's mama
but the old crone, she spoke so well
when little Joe said "Mommy, dear
I'm almost like the Tsar right now"
Legend has it that this legend coughed
shook her death-bed head and stammered forts:
boy, you should have become a priest

And well, who am I to disagree?
there would have been some Georgian scandals
because that boy was fucking crazy
but maybe, just maybe not
the founding of an Evil Empire
In the same way, shape or form

and I don't know what a KGB counsellor
could have told Vladimirovich
Maybe months after East Berlin
he held his post and Moscow was silent
and he had to do something other

than just obey pre-paid orders

but maybe just like mama Ketevan Geladze
someone should have told Putin
boy, you can be anything!
just do not be the absolute Tsar

tyrants falls, as Gandhi said
often while digging their own grave
if you breed a gangster country
gang-logic will follow you

and it's money talks,
respect and Glory
translated into strange new-fascism
that makes up gangster languages
Tito is said to have answered Stalin
in a late 40's official letter
in a Godfather-kind-of-way
which is cool if you think it's cool
but at the same time,

Stop sending people to kill me. We've already captured five of them, one of them with a bomb and another with a rifle. If you don't stop sending killers, I'll send one to Moscow, and I won't have to send a second…

is not peace, love and understanding
is not something to build a world on
is not bridges between countries and people

it's not, exactly, *the dog's bollocks*

back to the Autumn storm
in my head that early, tall September
with my synapses filled with info
from the grand old Per Arne Bodin himself
I walked around the campus's site
saw the clear autumn sky
and my ex wasn't there, and I was free
my new life cookin' and a brewin'

I thought I caught a crescent glimpse
of the soul of Mother Russia
there are gold there, and greatness, calm
domes and steppes and Circassian culture
great distances, inherited
ideas and people
and beautiful struggles

but then there is the mud and blood
the *Sonderweg* so unfathomable
the hatred, memory, the heavy amnesia
that only time, options and very good
forces must find quick (not easy)
ways to unfold and walk

as Putin goes the Way of Tyrants
other bricks fall down in some Othello
game with effects of dominoes
that remain obscure and volatile

figures like Ramzan Kadyrov
Rasputin, Lenin and Mr Stalin himself
strange Fools in Christ, I'll tell you that
it's a shame they get so much power

I want to swoon at that Autumn sky
imagine a future Russia
a Russia welcomed into EU, or something
living up to it's widened steppes
its domes of gold and beautiful struggles
finding the span that is a worthy *Sonderweg*
up to happiness as the world burns
like a rotisserie-chicken, set aflame

Antennas of the Antilles

The conquerors nurtured a deadly desire for gold and silver in the mines of the New World. They laid siege to the coast, then the forest, then the Andes and the High Plateaus with its abandoned cities. They devastated the surrounding in their prurient and maddening mystical rage. Tragic Love song with the new land. Increased advances, massacre, final solitude. A breaking is fulfilled; but Man will not give up his dream. He repopulates what he has depopulated. Plundering followed by plundering. The different names of the Conqueror: Cortez, Pizarro, Almagro, Balboa. The mad killer: father Valverde. The one he baptizes, and the one he strangles: Atahualpa, the last lover of the red earth.

– Édouard Glissant

I. Albion

The octopus of the seven oceans
the tentacles, the greedy hands
like prints from World War Number One
where the German Kaiser turned wild gorilla
strangles the world with bloodied hands

the cotton, tea, sugar, salt, the coffee
the pineapples on special holders
the rising Victorian luxury
your Laura Ashley of olden days
adored, admired, put on shelves
still remains a power symbol
– in those glossy posh magazines–
the pith helmets, the peacock feathers
deer antlers, narwhals, ivory horns
who are such a breed of people
to call others beasts, cockroaches, monkeys
when you have forsaken humanity
in favor of slavery and whips?
just to test the loyalty
of the army in India
didn't you make special shells
consisting of pork– and beef
so that when you were to reload
you had to pick them with your mouth
just to maximize the humiliation
of the Muslims and Hindus alike?
even if that's an urban myth

you cannot ever joke away
the Amritsar, the Zulu-massacres
if you ever do such a thing
you are hardly human anymore
you've traded your humanity
for something I dare not name

best parliamentary system ever?
what about the two-party bickering?
the monopolizing power?
your representation quotas?
your colonial protectorates?
those stupid little fucking wigs?
the wars that Maggie Thatcher fought?
against IRA and Argentina?
your royalties, your House of Lords?
your own country-club the Commonwealth?
the fact that you killed all the British bees?

what exactly is so heavenly?
and what are you afraid of, *sir*?
The Revenge that will come to you?
for making trades with human cargo?
when Big Brother USA won't help?
and you have burned your EU-bridges?
losing Northern Ireland
Scotland,
Wales?
what will remain then, football-violence?
Shepherd's pie, crumpets, bowling lawns?

you're not even best at cricket!
Australia, India, The Caribbean
have won the World Cup more times than you

Winston Churchill-nostalgias
when you shout out that awful anthem
Rule Britannia, Britannia rule the world
why are you so afraid?

England never ever shall be slaves,
right?

II. Gallia the "great"

The guillotine Empire
what's making us laugh so hard
is that you really seem to think
that you are out there civilizing
you put a ban on sex with minors
anno domini 2021
you still hit your children last I looked
and you've got *over sea territories*
legally a part of France
I almost want to stop right there

but there never were no dominatrix
giving you your punishment
pay you back for the Napoleon wars
the Sun King and the Revolution
never meant for more than white-skinned
Robespierre-types-of-gentlemen
and other hook-and-ladder-lads
swearing in to make their takeover
at the Oath at the Tennis Court
Fourth Republic Yugo-nostalgia:
Charles de Gaulle was a war criminal
Fight-to-the-death-crazy-in-the-head
Just a few pinnacles above
Pétain in Vichy sittin' pretty
and wanna know what I think about
your peculiarism, your snobbism
your arrogance and pseudo-smartness
your Jean Claude Arnault-culture?
I dislike that shit so much!

III. Hesperia

sometimes I think your kind of evil
your Catholic, Spanish, hardcore-evil
Castellistic, Carlistic, Falangistic
Franco-ism, inquisition-ism
your moral mongering war-torn crumbling
language murdering and landscape-raping
evil is the worst of all

fucking climate changes caused by you
because so many people died
in what became Latin-America
and you began the concentration camps
in Cuba back in the days
post-Columbus and the Caribs
but pre-Castro and pre-Che Guevara
never been a Fidel-fan
and I would not rock the t-shirt either
of Ernesto Che Guevara
but it would not have come down to that
unless you first had exterminated
the Caribs and the other tribes
from the Andes to the Great Antilles
New Mexico to Mexico
renamed Abya Yala
and shoved your language down its throat

you shot José Martí
you shot Julio Antonio Mella

and in the battle of Ayacucho
did you wave the white flag in peace?
don't forget Batista either
he got to land in soft Marbella
Cortez, Magellan, Pizarro
you yourself know the list too well
from Ferdinand and Isabella
to Franco and his Carmen Polo
dirty wars and coup d'états

sometimes I'm thinking that your evil
your cutthroat, brutal, Spanish evil
Carlistic, Falangistic, Catholic
Franco-istic, inquisition-esque
moral mongering, all-out plundering
evil is the worst of all

IV. The Monarchy of Modern Sweden

Our chains proved the very best
Swedish iron held the slaves, the finest
quality of iron ore
our sturdiness in exporting iron
steel and later guns and bombs
is really a metaphor
for the soul of our monarchy
we never need to pull the trigger
for that, there are other murderers
but the cluster-bombs, the chains for slaves
Gustavia and Guadeloupe
Saint-Barthélemy, hypocrisy
the subduing and the abuse and terror
of Sápmi and half the Baltic Sea
with Poland being the only country
mentioning Sweden in their national anthem
surprise: not that much good to say
the fifth columnism, the idleness
says Made in Sweden, yells it out
in big fucking capital letters

V. Winds gaining the upper hand

But the Antilles have got antennas
and in every direction now
thumps rhythms
from other drums
storms form now
in other's makings
that means winds
that gain the highest strength, the upper hand
dear Lords
Sires, Men of West
High Queens
of Babylon
Madame Colonialist
Sir Mr No Perspective
Señor death-from-a-muzzle-flame
you won't win the sweepstakes then

Who took the trans (out of transcendence)?

–questions through Shakespeare, Little Richard, Jesus and Van
"The Man" Morrison

Through the X:s and the Y:s
defecation in the eyes
pushed out through a narrow vault
we were born, wasn't our fault

(Some believe: by a Loving Lord)

I was one week old, couldn't write
speak, walk or tell left from right
a creature (though magnificent)
could not sign my birth certificate

(My name; the gift, me: the recipient)

"God made him, and therefore let him pass for a man."
   — Portia, 1.2.59

I've sat in temples, felt the calm
Christian, Judaism, Islam
Buddhist, Hindu, *Folkets Hus*
the same kind of collective *rus*

(In Sweden, God means Gud)

And I've studied what Jesus said

according to the Bible-scribes, the bread
and the fishes, and the cures
I see the example, the allure

(To rest in faith upon the Lord)

You ain't supposed to hide nothing—you've got it. God gave it,
show it to the world!
–Little Richard

If you believe in a loving God
who's ideas, facing a mob
of scared opponents, like in Rome
martyred, but retaliation – no

(that deserves some kind of throne)
But what throne are you sitting on
when you see beauty, rising strong
in flair and feathers, gladness, song
and condemn those you deem wrong

(For simply being trans and born)

"I am a Jew. Hath not a Jew eyes? Hath not a Jew hands, organs,
dimensions, senses,
affections, passions; fed with the same food, hurt with the same
weapons, subject to the same diseases, healed by the same means,
warmed and cooled by the same winter and

summer as a Christian is? If you prick us do we not bleed? If you
tickle us do we not laugh? If you poison us do we not die? And if
you wrong us shall we not revenge?"
  — Shylock, 3.1.60–70

It's not a lifestyle, preferred choice
of course boys would still be boys
and ditto girls, if it felt right
but people have always seen the light

(And have had their souls ignite)

In many cultures, except ours
transgenders have been rendered Gods
and that is *not* the roles we seek
we are of humankind, and meek

(Cut us open, and we bleed)

"The devil can cite Scripture for his purpose."
  — Antonio, 1.3.99

Carved out of Great Nature, then
came the cherished Children of Men
with all the lions, lambs, the wren
all the *han,* and *hon,* and *hen*

(We all are part of one big zen)

It's not a prayer, not a plea

for we do still exist, you see
you cannot wish us all away
that's only devil-spread decay

(Jesus would have loved *Born this way*)

Judge not, that ye be not judged
–Matthew, 7:1

The regret-rate is one percent
transgender-operations, they repent
because, in the final, bitter end
their peers would not let them in, accept

(Regret-rate is fifty percent
by gastric-bypass patients
and they get praised, life can commence
we could make that true for us as well)

And as we came marching publicly
declaring our Love and Pride
crowds cheered, only the Nazis brooded
and people waving the Virgin Bride

(Screaming loudly how Jesus loved us
if we just crawled back to hide)

So sad to see the maddened crowd
waving portraits of a man
who just said "love thy neighbor"

using his name to condemn trans

(If you believe in a God of Love
why would you clench an opened hand)

So when they continued asking him, he lifted up himself, and said
unto them, he that is without sin among you, let him first cast a
stone at her.
–John, 8:7

I believe I've transcended
I believe I've transcended
–Van Morrison, Astral Weeks (Live)

Women in America

Women in America
walks in hard places, receiving rocks
supposed to be an effeminate
mother of a godlike goddess
possess the courage of Miss Sarajevo
of 1993 in that cellar
be a sassy, caring, loving best-friend-trope
allowing girlfriends to maintain lead role-status
in their lives yet maintaining ownership of one's own
and she's set to be a savvy business entrepreneur
hold no bodily liquids, spill no tears of joy
consume nothing, yet everything
and at any teeny tiny transgression
the hammer strikes the anvil,
hard.

Women in America
are still being groomed
all the way up to the altar
when Daddy gives them a new Daddy
a purchase of the patriarchy

Women in America
are under attack from grim harvest reapers
devouring embryos
placing un-life over actual life
for their evil, bloated, asylum-insane
craze of a power tantrum

insane plots to enslave femme-coded bodies
invoking the Holy Lord as divine aid
the most twisted religion
even Jesus must've heard about

Women in America
are not even in America
they float on the continent
named Turtle Island
(Khéya Wíta in the Lakota language
Ragwis Yuwena in Tuscarora tongue)
inhabited by 8 or 10
different cultural spheres
with hundreds of tribes
hundreds of languages
still echoing, winning the war for them
Navajo Windtalkers encrypting commandos
that the Germans couldn't understand
saving world peace, democracy
and throwing women back into the kitchen
which the war-economics 1910's and 1940's
had catapulted them right out of
so came the 50's, 80's, came today

Women in America
so brave, diverse and beautiful
ordeals are sometimes just ordeals
and we learn nothing at all from them
but other times (and I think this is one)
you learn that it is together

victories has been won in the past
and in order for rectification
we need a thing called Sisterhood
the good thing is, it is already practiced
amongst mothers, sisters, lovers, friends
in a micro-scale like silent prayers
every place where two women meet

Women in America:
all continents are on your side
to craft your armor as the Dark rises

PART II:
CARIBBEAN WIND (MINES OF GENDER DYSPHORIA)

Did you ever have a dream, that you couldn't explain?
Ever met your accusers, face to face in the rain?
I see the screws breakin' loose, see the devil pounding on tin
I see a house in the country being torn apart from within
I can hear my ancestors calling from the land far beyond

And them Caribbean winds still blow from Nassau to Mexico
Fanning the flames in the furnace of desire
And them distant ships of liberty on them iron waves so bold and free
Bringing everything that's near to me nearer to the fire

-Bob Dylan

Two Rivers (Fertile Crescents ascending)

Ashes to ashes, dust to cold call ground
Euphrates and Tigris are the choices *du jour*
or I mean who am I kidding, no choices prevail
you were kinda Cain-branded from the day you were born
one sign for Male, one for Female

The Babylonian narrative is obsolete bullcrap
we could do so much better, and we're aware that we can
we shouldn't swallow the tackle, buy ready-made products

such as skirts/tender/pink/female, blue/power/force/man

A woman in Slovenia, she just shook her head at me
in Greece a woman let the shit hit the fan
I did not master the language, the symbols, the letters
couldn't read the signs reading woman and man

Primary schools fight to ban stoves to play with
So that young girls won't be tethered to them
but the boys play with guns, being genocide champions
being cowboys and "Indians", plucking feathers from them
we play cops and Batman, play princes and orcs
then the kids go and become the world, witches are torched
we pretend that some will perish while others will prevail
some we teach to be male, others we assign female

I may be analphabetic but the genders are floating
words become blurs and water turns wine

feel like an oarsman, saddled up, going boating
like I pick up my shovel and walk to the mine
I go downtown in clouds of jealousy tearing my heart up
it bothers me while I'm working, it's kind of a pain
I know I'm not my dysphoria, but it rattles my cart, rough
it never grows soft in me; it stands where it stands
on the devil's crossroads right 'tween woman and man

but like in some love story or a tale about rivers
the rivers shall meet and make fertile crescents
Euphrates and Tigris supporting each other
make alliances, forge bonds and together ascend
new seed planted in the soil, new strength to guide them
strong compasses encompass what they will and they can
she lets him in her circles, he learns to confide in them
and we redraw the patterns of Woman and Man

Avatar

Choose your password and username
It must contain the following:
at least a few letters, right?
gotta have some syllables
it don't mean a thing if it ain't got that swing
please lord let it be fool-proof-strong
make it work in every room and place
throw in some mandatory vowels

how to navigate the ebbs and flows?
there are quite a few languages
and a lot of them syllables
most of them can steer you wrong

Khaleesi became popular
a Game of thrones-name on coded girls
newborn girls in the US of A
because... I guess... the lack of?
female role models, protagonists
in the land where some Daddy's still
ceremonially "gifts" the bride
to the bride groom like some offering
to the Moloch of patriarchy
in the name of holy matrimony

but behold, Khaleesi made a mess
spoiler alert but she turned bad
and the inboxes filled up with errants
renaming the little ones

in the year 1945
Adolf wasn't all that popular

So, choose your name carefully Arvida
can you wield it through storms?Juni
stand up for your avatar?Svenske

The drug of being good

We, the privileged with stacks of status
power, money, cultural capital
the right contacts
the right education.
We, who do not have to beg
for others to save our lives
we, who have attained and bred
house ownerships, blond little children
we hereby hold the microphone
wanting to throw a house party!
with all you lovely little rascals
representatives of multi-culti!
You know, you guys
are the rising rainbow
we
are just the plain salad
we've discussed in certain study groups
in suburbs oh so pretty green
and also, one downtown, know what I mean?
I actually took the bus that day
(such a goddarn pretty little sight!)
(it felt like going out abroad!)
(Arabia, Polynesia,
The West Indies, The Middle East!)
(you know, once, I was in Africa
they got such cool, pretty, funky, viby
cloths and patterns and dances there!
we have got a lot to learn

from the foods of other cultures
ours are so dull and boring
and we put ours in senior housing
but they care about good old Grandma...)

we were wrong, sorry, not sorry!
we want to understand even more.
we've been stupid like a prejudice!
we want to understand so much better
understand what you're going through
hand me those shoes of yours!
I'll walk two full miles in it (I've ran marathons, you know)
and together we will raise money (strike that) awareness!
far beyond the height of Babel's tower.

We want to share and have ears big like trolls
to hear some other, new, fresh perspective
some raw, spicy, lime perspective
that clears the mind and broadens all.
Follow us on Instagram
let's crowdfund the whole thing up
let's make a great big potluck, y'all
don't forget to pay for membership
and RSVP ten days ahead

Ögon känsliga för grönt (Eyes sensitive to green)

There's a picture of Hispaniola
where Haiti meets the Dominican
republic and you see the difference
on the Dominican side your eyes can see
roads winding green and forest-like
patterns swell and there's harmony
but on the side of poor Haiti
it's a Mordor-waste of deforestation
dirt roads and muddy stumps

to me, that's like clothing stores
you've got a sea of meadow flowers
forms, shapes, skirts and dresses
in the colors of all Ethiopia
and you've got the Grey Area
with tones of black, blue and brown
flannel, suits, ties and fads
tense and tight and Nordic cool
I was banished there throughout my life

to a no-mans-land of Hispaniola
colonially burnt to dust
to maintain a rigid role
keep up appearances from the sugar fields
but I was just going around feeling:
gimme some sugar man!

but respite is not given to

a coded boy trekking across the borders
it becomes a chore, a boring job
and you start to not give a damn

they burn you down throughout your teens
and it takes years to renew crops
especially if you don't want to grow
the same old boring mono-culture

the point is not to hammer down
the pain of poor Arvida here
but I mean the metaphor
holds up, because we don't grow the crops
the Global North wear the cotton
the Global South picks and colors it
and all your scraped-out Acne-jeans
someone has had to scrape them out

there's a picture of Hispaniola
showing gender grey and green
but like Barbro Hörberg sang
det var ett egendomligt ljus den dagen

Gillette (the best a man can get)

some kind of wonderful
on the other side of loneliness
the end of what is known as boyhood
the embryo of what we call manhood

when I started to grow stubbles
I got to hear, all of a sudden
that I was upgraded to be a man

almost like a rite of passage
my father oozed of manly pride
when I got to learn the craft
(just like in some old commercial)
how to stand in front of your reflection
meet your scared little avatar
stare into your soul's vacuum
draw razors across your cheeks

the best a man can get

is that really razors
though?

I wouldn't say I actually
seriously considered it
but once when I was just thirteen
the thought struck me as I looked around
that if I died no one would miss me

that razors were the best thing
a man could ever get

of course, there is some cotton candy
fabric softeners and little precious
emerald-jewels here and there
but when I'm being spontaneous
exactly what's good about manliness?

The list does not become that long

But tenderness and strength get in
comradeship and playfulness
kindness and supportiveness
passing of knowledge, loyalty
and respect, if you define it right

but I would guess it's safe to say
razors do not make the list

Pre-op voodoo blues

So you can stick your little pins in that voodoo doll
I'm very sorry, baby, doesn't look like me at all

-Leonard Cohen

Up on the podium's just a shell of me
the remains of me that is a man
the remnants of my older self
beautiful like a stale train station
from some worn-down empire
and still possessing the glow
posing for the clay-ladies
remainder-Arvid standing there
naked as the course participants
looks in deep concentration
total focus, zero sexuality
at Åke Hans, Bredgatan 5, Lund
where August Strindberg used to get drunk

for structure and for formatting
the silence is pierced by them
smashing clay against the working spaces
they stick pins in for stability
for the clay figure to stand up straight
an effigy, not really me
but still, pretty grotesque to think
a needle straight through your head

somebody else being chiseled forth
becomes some new Prometheus
but I have found my imperishable flame
I'm Embla, not Ask, you know
Eve and not Adam now
Narai is me, and not Maono
that is the true shape of my heart
Caribbean winds brought me there
and many hard and winding waves
but I find peace in paddling
I will make it to distant shores

She rises (she bangs)

Does my sexiness upset you?
Does it come as a surprise
That I dance like I've got diamonds
At the meeting of my thighs?

–Maya Angelou

She rises,
blossoms,
thrives,
and swells
the function of a wave
and its everliving love-affair
with the Beach
Of Life.
She rises, gushes forwarding, cascadingly,
she bangs.

Out of all the blue of history
the haze slowly vanished
the sheets and covers of erasure
removed quilt by tiny quilt
Women throughout history
has always been everywhere
not always in a warrior stance
but always protecting Life
not always taking seven-mile strides
but always making all the differences

Oh baby,

when she moves,
she moves

I go crazy 'cause she looks like a flower
And like a flower (like a fruit) is often measured by
The amount of juice it can produce
Squished in some Joe and The Juice-cocktail
I go crazy, because there's so many flowers
trampled under foot, and withered
women all around the world:
you are so goddamn beautiful
not by mere looks (but you're pretty too)
but by being so much *humans*
humane, firm, feminine
#fightlikeagirl

not sharpening knives
to be waging a war
but for the eventuality
of both carving wood,
preparing food,
cutting through textiles
and protecting the ones she loves
whenever men go against her
she preserves life like a flower
But she stings like a bee

Like every girl in history

reminds me that a woman's got one thing on her mind:

jeans with pockets, equal rights for all.

Open letter to JK Rowling (and her likes)

You're gonna die who you are. So you have to constantly work on
who you are, so that the stars align correctly.
– man on the Angie Martinez show

You used to be the cool Mum
teach kids to
stick it to the Man, stick to your friends
kill the Voldemort
strength in unity,
but diversity…
not anymore.

Being transgender is being horrocruxed
into pieces by the likes of you
Death-eater, fascist-complier
Holocaust-denier, *et tu Brute*-brute.
You've lost a fan through thorough hatred.

If I have children
They won't get to hear Harry Potter.
read aloud by my beautiful trans-woman-voice
through my trans-woman-feminine-lips
flipping pages with my trans-woman fingers
reading to my beautiful rainbow children
who will be taught *you can be what you are*
and love *those your heart yearns to.*
And *stand up to fucking fascists.*

You sort of kind of Frankenstein'ed
But you yourself became the monster
When you entered Whacko-La-La Land
Became the prime mayor of Crazy Town
Took the TERF-crown and paraded it
Well, congratulations, Miss Universe
biggest hater of all the planets
lined up in the Milky Way
sick, venal like the streets of New York
Robert de Niro rages on in Taxi Driver
that's how your sectarian anti-trans mafia
seems to all of us, in the normal world.

Who hurt you, really, who hurt you?
And is this really healing on your part somehow?
Enough of all this vitriol.
Let's get back to the program here.
I believe I was writing poetry.

*Transgender women are women. Any statement to the contrary
erases the identity and dignity of transgender people and goes
against all advice given by professional health care associations
who have far more expertise on this subject matter than either Jo or
I. According to The Trevor Project, 78% of transgender and
nonbinary youth reported being the subject of discrimination due
to their gender identity. It's clear that we need to do more to
support transgender and nonbinary people, not invalidate their
identities, and not cause further harm.*
*I am still learning how to be a better ally, so if you want to join me
in learning more about transgender and nonbinary identities check*

out The Trevor Project's *Guide to Being an Ally to Transgender and Nonbinary Youth*. It's an introductory educational resource that covers a wide range of topics, including the differences between sex and gender, and shares best practices on how to support transgender and nonbinary people.

To all the people who now feel that their experience of the books has been tarnished or diminished, I am deeply sorry for the pain these comments have caused you. I really hope that you don't entirely lose what was valuable in these stories to you. If these books taught you that love is the strongest force in the universe, capable of overcoming anything; if they taught you that strength is found in diversity, and that dogmatic ideas of pureness lead to the oppression of vulnerable groups; if you believe that a particular character is trans, nonbinary, or gender fluid, or that they are gay or bisexual; if you found anything in these stories that resonated with you and helped you at any time in your life — then that is between you and the book that you read, and it is sacred. And in my opinion nobody can touch that. It means to you what it means to you and I hope that these comments will not taint that too much. Love always,

–Daniel Radcliffe

For Elliot

and trans-men across the world

Lovely
lovely Elliot
I saw the news today.

I loved you in June
in In love with Rome
and I saw the news today.

Joy fills me like a tired sunrise
an exciting ascending star
or the
coming out of a shower
after a workout
and you're just enough
exhausted
but *the yawns are smiles,*
you know?

Elliot, it's not going to get easier
but you are going to be less alone.

And I do believe, in my experience

being a boy, you know, and all

I would hate that for me

but I love that for you.

Lovely
lovely Elliot.
I heard the news today.

Non-binaries, gender-fluids

You
are
The
Crack
in
everything.

You're
where
The Light
gets in.

Thank you for the refuge

to Lou and the crew of fantastic people in and around Page 28 in Malmö

Thank you for the refuge
from the roads and from the world
back when life was turmoil
and I was neither boy nor girl

thank you for the painted floors
of lavender and white
thank you for bringing ghosts to life
and turning them to cheerful sprites

thank you for the fairies
the pixies and the fairytales
the beardless males and females
the hairy females, hairy males

thank you for the in-between
the space, the air, the view
thanks for nurturing That Feeling
and for helping me staying true

thanks for the asexual
who do not lust for flesh
thanks for ancient knowledge
deeper than the Gilgamesh

thank you for the haven

down by northern Charles' Crown's Square
thank you for the purple light
I do believe that light is rare

Thank you for the book clubs
the circles made us wise
sometimes some sprinkled fairy dust
just makes your life suffice

Thank you for your standing days
in the Mitt-i-Möllan-market-bustle year
Mothership, I believed you've anchored
you've made your harbour here

Thank you for the refuge
one Easter Saturday
that could have been a deluge
of the inner matter clay

Thank you from a refugee
in the Gender Wars of yorn
emerging from the rubble
in a dress that's torn and worn

Saying grace to Page 28
Thank you,
sages of Page 28
mages of Page 28
graces of Page 28
may age never grow on Page 28

Octopuses playing harpsichords

Everything that is visible hides something that is invisible.

–René Magritte

We are octopuses playing harpsichords
so much defines us: by our heart's accord
and by our actions, memories, words and friends
we will be judged, remembered near the end

I'm not just a woman, trans-dito, lover, friend
poet, writer, teacher, daughter, trend
tax-payer, fellow human, samaritan
star-dust, celestial child and fan

Of Star Wars, Astrid Lindgren, Tolkien, J.R.R
of music, books, and paint, and art
who's got a lot of tiny pains and scars
who's kind and sweet, vain, Venus, Mars

Gender is just one identity
inexhaustible resource, grows on plenty trees
just pick one up and try it on for fun
if you don't like it– try another one

We are octopuses playing harpsichords
displaying new sides when our hearts are sore
carnivorous mammals bred on mother's milk
who walks in rags and skirts and silk

Don't judge Tȟuŋkášila Šákpe by her four ugly guys
the Mt Rushmore-ugly blemish on the South Dakotan
countryside
we all are steeped in history but in such different, un-funny
ways
octopuses playing harpsichords neath' a fiery light-bulb's
sunny rays

History without discomfort is propaganda.

–Fellowship Congregational United Church of Christ (of all
places!)

Caribbean wind

The first day I want out wearing a dress
nothing special about that day
it was June, and it was very soft
how the wind was playing with the fields

took the same bus I always do
sat down on nearly the same seat
thought I wore make-up enough kill a boar with
but really, just a thin layer
of foundation and some velvet lip gloss

I spoke to Saga on the phone
and no one said anything
not for, not against, you see
they probably thought of things you do
when you tend to take the bus
on a day in June 2019
line 171 to Lund

a ray of sunshine through the window
as I sat in therapy
then I remember how the wind
conspiratorial and satyr-like
sassy and almost flirting
whispered me my one true name

it said Arvida,
pled Arvida

bled Arvida,
spread Arvida
get fed, Arvida!
go ahead Arvida!
I remember when I read
Arvida

And I remember falling from the sky
With our bird of steel from the USA
Miami, FLA
reaching Norman Manley International
November 2015, Kingston, Jamaica

I did not possess the language then
Not the tools nor the nuances
but then wind that was blowing then
felt warm and caring, caressing, Caribbean
and I knew it when it came back
blowing softly that day in June
when I went out in my pink silk dress
tasting a name that's true to me

the guide at the Bob Marley-museum
said of rain that it's like *liquid sunshine*
who are we to not presume
that everybody's genderfluid
that it is just different
stadiums, phases, strings on a large harp
different stages of aggregation
sometimes frozen, sometimes steam

and sometimes just a human wave
in Kingston Harbour, Caribbean
the wind's direction doesn't matter
every ocean shares the water
the waves that fondle Port of Spain
also caress the Baltic Sea

PART III:
POLYNESIAN STORM- OR A STORM WITH A FEMALE NAME

Storm is a wind measuring 24,5 and 28,4 m/s or 11 beaufort. A storm is formed in the disruption of the zone separating hot and cold air and in stark temperature contrasts. The weather phenomenon happens both at sea and on land. On land, storms can uproot trees and cause damages to houses. At sea, the winds can cause high tidal-waves. The surface goes white from the heavy foam. The Swedish Meteorological and Hydrological Institute used WMO: recommendation about giving, naming one storm female and the next male.

– trans woman and activist Saga Becker reading out of her interpretation on Swedish Weather Institute SMHI's information text about Storms.

We came to this world to make it another world.

– Paulo Freire

Children on the plaid

There is social service-picture
that just don't give me any rest
the man asked us about the way
the accent was Persian

the social services had called him there
and he just couldn't reach the appointment late
because they would decide
his future for the upcoming time
the GPS on his cellular phone
suddenly died and he needed to
restart the applications
that's when I saw his screensaver

The children lay upon the plaid
couldn't even be two years old
twins needed to be kept alive
it was them he attended meetings for

and so parents have always needed
to go to battles like lions do
to fight like mother-tigers do
raise their offsprings to the sky like Simba
(metaphorically) and bring them life

And I'm thinking if that Dad has taken
his family from Khamenei's killers
he should possess the longevity

to battle
Swedish social service
But it's just
Another type of violence I guess

The children laid upon the plaid
in cabins when Gustav Vasa
burned down almost all of Småland
when men with names like Bougainville
Cook, Cortez, Columbus
came with sicknesses and death-sentences
when Hitler plagued continents
Napoleon plagued continents
Queen Victoria plagued continents
when slaves would extract resources
from the mines and the cotton-fields
and when Alberto Fujimori
and his governmental task-forces
hunting down the communist
of Sendero Luminoso
would torch half the Andes down

Children would lay down on the plaids
and most of them survived

Tourists of Existence

May 2021

through Konstantin Kavafis Refugees

October 1914

It's still Malmö. If you use the old
apostle horses, leave the Central station
take that street that has the Hippodrome
go toward the Calender of Light, enter the Castle Park
and you will find keeps and monuments that astonishes you.
Seek the beach in twilight on a trans-colored summer's day
and I will show you a crescent of happiness.
No matter how the gang violence rages
or how it's portrayed in the media,
it remains a lovely little city.
and time passes
calm like a fed canine
when you're field tripping
reading books and doing different studies.

The nights we gather on the beach
(all of us bearing different names)
and look with strange reverence
at the turquoise, pink and red and yellow
Summer Straight blessing Copenhagen.
They're not in vain! No, they're very useful
to pluck out from the memory bank

when November haunts the souls
and we, that remained in the city
remained in the city.

Sometimes we talk about things we never dared
(they seem a bit more down to earth here)
sometimes of the ephemeral and ethereal.
I read Konstantin Kavafis
two days ago, it took until now
for his poem to find my soul.

Such pictures, such rhythm, such clearness, such harmony.
In my corona-intoxicated state
I stare as wide-eyed as a headlight-deer
unto an October-poem from 1914. 2021 now, the calendar
fills up with distances and cancellations
but the same refuge, same refugees, same Mediterranean Sea
same border trades and military forces
to fence out those we don't want to let in.

And we perceive the weakness, oh but the migrant's
strength
travelers not on some dull journey
we meet them with a measured nod
maintaining our skeptical composure
towards these heroes of surviving life.

Yet we are all but the same
summer organism under the sun
those nights when the beach has called us

(all of us bearing different names)
and look with strange reverence
at the pink, turquoise, red and yellow
Summer Straight blessing Copenhagen.

You can always translate a sunset.
Thus, the days go by, these times are not
boring because this too shall pass
it will not always be like this.
Nothing but good news, either we are
in the right type of vaccine-group
or we just have to hold our breath some more.
Something will lighten up in Syria
in Yemen too, and Ethiopia
peace in Congo and South Sudan
a new Egypt treasuring its treasures
well, maybe even Malmö city
can be the Mecca of multiculturalism
the tourist guides claim it already is.

Then, dear friends, my heart bleeding, beating for you,
your time will finally arrive.

Chorus of the corals
(Dog whistles from the depths)

Sometime in the grey dawn of the primeval times, the first seed of life had come with the sun down to the desolate vastness of the underwater. Down to the silent depths the light reached out. Down there sunrays strayed, that would warm and encourage every living thing. And life grew. Everything moved and struggled. The existence of being changed and was renewed. And every morning new life streamed down from the sun– millennium followed millennium.

In the warm ocean the reef corals would toil. From the sea they received their nourishment. The sea gave them lime and pigmentation for their great constructions. In the form of coruscating reefs and giant-like pillars they reached the surface. They became sandy islands, transmuting through long times and harsh storms unto green, shimmering oases where Man and beast could live. Sometimes the coral would start their work at the bottom of the mountains down below. Sometimes they'd build on sinking islands. The corals would even up the movement downward. They built ever onwards, upwards. They were life, striving toward the light and warmth of the water's surface. They were the spawn of the sun-impregnated sea. On the stale craters of the sea-bottom the corals built their foundational walls around black abysses, holes who once belched out glowing mass in multitudes.

Other times, they'd build too early, before the eruptions had ended, before the volcanoes had finished shaping and molding the

*fundaments for the oncoming societies. For the collective peace-
work of the corals relied on the rock-hard exceptions, created
through the burning upheavals of nature. What did not rest upon
basalt as hard as flintstone – on the foundations of the fully fledged
Revolution– was doomed to die. See, it would waver when the
storm came. It would crack or burst into flames, set ablaze by the
rising firepower of the underworld.*

*But when the storm had stilled and the violent volcano had become
a safe, ready-cast base, new corals came back. They were travelling
pioneers, small flickering creatures from other creations. Before
they began their life-work they had the individual freedom to
choose their place. They settled down and began their toiling. Soon
towering, shiny walls rose in triumph, where their forefathers once
had failed. Always they fought. Steady their societies grew.
Constantly they had to shield themselves against the coming of the
wild currents. Always they would toil away, generation after
generation, always raising their buildings unto higher levels. Their
glittering walls became the largest constructions seen on Earth.*

*The corals worked together. This was their strength. Not just as
individuals but also as nations they cooperated. White and yellow,
red and blue, they all worked in harmony with each other. The reef
corals would build protective walls for the many-colored brothers
of the inner reef. Thanks to the bastion-workers the calm water
corals could grow their resplendent gardens. And all the
individuals and all the nations had the same goal: to build and to
stick together. Only by doing that they would survive. They all
would strive to climb from the darkness, up toward the light,
onward to the sun. For they loved him. It was him; he had fertilized*

the ocean. With his beams, life-seeds flowed down into the opaque green. With his beams, the longing for eternity had come to the desolation of the primeval sea.

-Sverre Holmsen retelling a Polynesian creation myth in *Sjungande korall* (Singing coral)

I've been listening to all the dissension
I've been listening to all the pain
And I feel that no matter what I do for you
It's going to come back again
But I think that I can heal it
But I think that I can heal it
I'm a fool,
but I think that I can heal it
with this song

-Leonard Cohen, Minute prologue

Like dog whistles in deep ocean
fragments of a monument
it took us (as per usual)
only a couple of
decades to tear it down

(a dog whistle in comparison:
while Reagan roared *tear down this wall*
Trump screamed about death penalty
in local papers back in 89′
fast forward: choirs of "build that wall!"

and US democracy
after four years of dismantling
it was ready to burn, burn, burn
like dry kindle in the sun)

the theory goes as follows:
Deep Hope is its elegant name
protection theory, *puipuiga manatu*
teoría de la protección, call it whatever
it claims the whole of the reef's alive
all the reef, down to the bottom
the corals are the reef's life-blood
so to speak its reservoir of life
from the Surface to the mesopelagic
twilight zone where nothing grows
except the corals of perpetual night
and the reef can be built from down there
when deep-sea corals rise and shine
to the light, warmth and love of Surface
they can repopulate the reefs like that
in a way we need so desperately
a recolonisation
from the sea we have colonized

and I didn't know all this until
I saw a French documentary
where they descended 170 meters
with rebreather and protective gear
and the courage of a hundred lions
they moved through these twilight worlds

their vessels laboratories
new corals, species, lifeforms, life
all showing in their deep-sea cameras
desolate much like Makatea
an atoll arisen, a fortress of the deep blue sea
housing mines that yielded phosphate
1917-66'
now only scarce vegetation
hides the phosphate scars given
it looked like a lunar landscape
like the Sea of Tranquility

a monument to French colonialism
with none of Jacques Cousteau's colors
in the twilight zone, the depths below
grey school sharks patrolled the night
the light decreased, the dark increased
light and temperature-sensitive lenses
to even mirror this twilight world
the divers wore these high-tech eyes
of Man pushing further into
the underworld Polynesia
colonies of Deep-sea corals
in plenitudes never seen before
the diver senses in full swing rockin'
the balance and the breathing
always the balance and the breathing

two and a half hours of decompression
to decrease the amount of helium

and nitrogen in the blood it takes
all that time to avoid Depth-sickness
see, in deep-sea diving there's a limit
not a depth-limit but the limit of Time
not the machines that limit us
but the fact that we are humans
it's the coldness, it's the fatigue

there's a standstill at six meters
Depth where Surface can be seen
you have to levitate there for hours
or blow up some vital organs
there is no way to bypass that

and when breaking new scientific
ground you have to be prepared
for things previously unseen

and then a horror-scene emerged
no Stephen King could ever write
a school shark in the mesopelagic
twilight world not adjusted to humans
these sharks have never seen
us strange half-monkeys there before
it suddenly swims in some strange-laid patterns
then BRUTALLY CHARGE at a diver's head
a cloud of blood from his helmet
it lets go and slips away
and he drops his rebreather
uses his bail-out oxygen-tank

succeeds in rising from the depths

but oh, must have been long hours
six feet Deep below that day
seeing the surface, aware a deep-sea shark
almost bit your head clean off
but he was not allowed to ascend
to the team to let them mend his head
he needed to levitate
six feet deep beneath the waves
for one hundred
and fifty minutes

there are befores
and there are afters
before   Maono would make sweet love
               the shark attack
after   to Narai in Makatea's caves
               the shark attack
before   and life itself sang to them
               the massive coral-death
after   under the magical sea-cave ceiling
               the Europeans came to stay
before   and the corals would sing to them
               there were resistance
after   the corals would sing to them
               we got organized

but there were also brutal beauty
corals lived there, and corals sang

a quiet hymn, inaudible
4 % of the total sunlight
they need to live and really grow
120 meter down
even deeper,
they also saw
life at 171 meters
under the Gambier-islands
no one has even seen before
it brings new light to the corals
and the data dwarfs the accident

and think of it, if there is life-hope
even in the purest pockets
of clinically dark deep-water
how much hope is not contained
in our *poches de résistance*
the sun even shines on us

and a man that was older than eighty
you know, a classic French scientist
first said with his *chercheur-voice*
how fantastic these findings were
then he broke down in quiet sobs
you know, when men who almost never cries
just let the tears come to them
in front of cameras, he said sorry
but I've been researching for sixty years
and I've never seen a thing like that

there are befores   Narai would give her love
and there are afters   to Maono in Makatea's caves

the dog whistles from the depths under the magic sea-cave
towering
if we listen closely, we may hear and life itself would sing to
them

(Beautiful but unattainable) refuge

It won't be the same Rangiroa.

- Bengt Danielsson

On an island in lake Nicaragua (also known as Cocibolca)
there are two majestic volcanos –
the active Concepción
the inactive Maderas.

Which of them stands for hope?
Which one stands for love?

Ometepe: a place of myth
since the pre-Columbian
civilizations of South America.

And there are many places just like that
most of them
remain a fantasy.

A most unattainable
refuge
beautiful
like a bowl of jade
among cotton clouds

when my ex and I were still together
we lived one bus station apart

in places called Ekhagen
and Stora Lappkärrsberget

among my most beautiful summers
burned into my mental gaze
I saw everything in new colors
as I wrote in my book at the time

it was like Narai and Maono
in the magic caves of Makatea
but no prophecy was fulfilled
no children, no heavy battles

and I could build monuments
hymns to Stora Lappkärrsberget
but time remains what it is

a beautiful but unattainable
refuge of days gone by

and Rangiroa and Tahiti
will always shine like stars above
like a kaleidoscope of dreams
our Dream-Tahiti, Vision-Tahiti
beautiful but unattainable
refuges from reality

Gale in my heart (Song in my head)

It almost requires
a pier, a jetty set in stone
or some other gazebo-point
overlooking the many oceans
remaining the same somehow
linked together by common streams
same Worldwind, same possibility
to make the human connection live
everywhere where waves come crashing
the ocean sings its mellow, wild, old song
some other Arvida dreams perhaps

dreamer like me, poet like me, mind-traveller like me
with the same awe and veneration
she sees the ocean that remains the keeper
of the minds and the memories
the whale-sharks and the warrior Orcas
the fishes and the many dreams

on Rarotonga and Suwarrow
Aitu and Manuae
Maute and Takutea
on Pitcairn, on the Line Islands
on Easter Island, Christmas Island
on Niue too, and on the Austral Islands
on Sala y Gómez too
on Tonga and on Tuvalu

dreamers like me, poets like me
same gazing eyes, same galing heart
the oceanic tumbling grounds
for dreams crushed and dreams regained
the whale-sharks and the giant sperm whales
the fishing fleets, the naval flags
the atolls and the concepts of Island
maybe just like some atomic egg
is brooding on the verge of hatching
to spread out bees and butterflies
flaming soft beads of flowers
that will scourge and embrace the world
in the warm love of all the world

I've stood and looked upon some oceans
The Andaman Sea, The Baltic Sea
The Atlantic gazing to the west
The Adriatic and the Indian Ocean
the endlessness of the Pacific
California only gave a hint

This is no simple name-and roll-call
and no, I won't ever seize to
write poems saying we are one
the oceans, stars, the skies up high
all of us with windy hearts
and songs rattling in our heads
one day we will raise our voices
in bitter enlightenment
and the song shall flow like breeze

the Sun go slowly on its way
like that time Maui wrestled with it
so his mother could hang her laundry
and dry them to become the clouds

maybe it's from Polynesia
that great storm is bound to come
I mean, Scania's fields are windy
and the dead winds packs a certain punch
and there's peace out on Österlen
in Stockholm and on Gotska Sandön
but seriously talking seriously now
it might not be here those winds occur
the one's sweeping the world in feminine
warmth and hugs Mother Earth.

Ink stains and untold stories

We Hawaiians believe the creation has two energies. The energies are called ku and hina. Ku is male energy, and hina is female energy. The dynamics between them has to be in balance. Otherwise, you're out of balance. You use tatau as a rite of passage to understand one's energies, and to make sure your energies balance each other. Every time you see the motive you've been given it is supposed to tell you what your mission is in life. We say that the pain you must endure when you receive a tatau fills the purpose of showing that life is painful and you have to work through it to live a rich life.

– Kahu Kauila Clark

Our motives were originally unruly and quite large. The reason being that we were a people of warriors. If you look up in the heat of battle and saw someone with very small tattoos you didn't know who it was. If you saw someone with big tattoos, you recognized them immediately.

– Keone Nunes

I grew up with a feeling of something missing. I took it upon myself to be the one to reclaim the knowledge and the one to link my family together with our history and culture.

– Kaipo Lindsey

The Master's Tools Will Never Dismantle the Master's House

– Audrey Lorde

I. Oahu

When you zoom in on the island, really *see* the nature
the stories and the tales of gods
come alive and breathe, they say
every hill, stone and forest clearing
has a name and a history
but it is not always held
behind lock and key by The Land Survey
with overview plans and resulting figures

Tattoos are not only markings
they are stories and old reminders
of the force of the striking thunder
the lean bodies of the lightning bolts
that the god Kāne brought with him
long before Liliʻuokalani
Kamehameha and the Wilcox rebels
the Bayonet Constitution and the Black Week
the Leper War and the takeover
in another time than Blue Hawaii
Apology Resolution?
make Puerto Rico a state already
the oldest tattoo-artist, Keone
on Waianae-coast of great Oahu
has five young apprentices
clearing the workspace for him
and creates all the tools from scratch
(in the same way as in the *olden times*
even the very same materials)
they stretch out the skin to paint upon

and make the master's day run smooth
every morning at four o'clock
just before the break of dawn
Keone walks down to the beach
and in an ancient ritual
he calls on the tools to wake
dipping them in the morning ocean
filling them with silent mana
gains the power to wield them right
the waves kiss and bless the tools
much as the waves have always done
and in the evenings when his work is done
he goes down to put them to sleep

Audrey Lorde, after all, said it best
the quote about the master's tool
and even more parts came together
when Keone explained his thoughts
for him, it all blended together
the Buddhism and the Hawaiian
sort of the same spiritual world
philosophy and way of life

look at something like *ala niho*
a tattoo-strip down across the leg
down to ankle-height
they make up unique stories
bearing up genealogy
and biological information
grants the bearer spiritual strength

Kaipo Lindsey said about Keone
he lives on another level
at the same time is the world we live in
and in the other, the spirit world
that hardly anybody knows about
with knowledges and great insights
far beyond our world's veil
when he meets people, he sees people
then he sees beyond them too
seeing their all their ancestors
where they came from, what their family did

you hear that being said of certain people
about some people it rings true

and a final food for thought I got
an *aloha* from Oahu
it's not just a way of greeting
it's a philosophical system
empathy, respect, and balance
and speaking of body love
a symmetric body
is to be a human
an asymmetric body
is to be a god
that is why tattoos are made
and so, dear friend
you just have to carry on
your cellulites, your flaws and stretch marks
makes you gods and goddesses

II. Samoa

– Your low, sharp, cutthroat canoes are bad ships. The rounded, voluptuous ships are better. Women aboard and banana-bundles in the back sparks joy. Ships with seeds and plants spread peace. Such vessels are welcome on Tahitian islands. Son of Taipi, tell all your chieftains that it would be wise for them to stop hunting "long swines". It would benefit the peace and their own wealth if they learned to fertilize instead of plundering, to give marotai instead of killing blindly.

– The Tahiti chieftain Maono's speech to a captured enemy-warrior of the Taipi-tribe, a tribe which according to the story clung to cannibalistic customs and had a ban on women in canoes. From Sverre Holmsens *Sjungande korall* (Singing coral).

What does being naked mean?
Naked in body, in thought, in life?
From Samoa a story reached me
Su'a Peter Sulu'ape said
that in the house of the highest chief
there is no taboo in nudity
at least not against exposing skin
but one that carries no tattoos
all the way down the chain of command
will not be granted entry there
because the body tells no stories

pe'a on men's upper body

malu on women's thighs
are ink stains and untold stories
uniting them and giving them strength

it used to be soot from burnt-down nuts
the mothers would start to gather
when a girl or a boy would come
mixed with holy sea-water
becoming ink stains and stories

Su'a Ala'vaa Petelo Sulu'ape
does not mix in that way anymore
with modern tools and pins and needles
the infection risk drops 50 percent
you still have to devote two weeks
several hours of each day
to lay still and the let needle work
to make the ink-stains tell its stories
the life-lines and the tales of forefathers
chiseled unto the bone-marrow

but he also says words of sorrow
standing in front in the camera crew
a bank of clouds darkening the sun
and he turns down his face and utters:

the connection to my ancestors...
it is as if I've lost it now

in a dream he saw a grand vision

where as many as possible
would be trained in the tattoo-arts
 "the traditional art of tattooing
in Samoa must survive and prosper
and continue until the world is ending"
and also like a quiet storm:
nobody can take it away from us

a painful birthday present given
a *tatau* gifted by your parents
like a final fare-thee-well
before you see the world in rovin' wonder

pe'a on men's upper bodies
malu on women's thighs
ink-stains telling tales and stories
marking and reminding you
to always expect the unexpected
see the Pole Star and the wondrous sky
remind yourself we all belong
to life together with everyone
that's ever lived or will be born
carry seeds on your life's canoe
make sure you plant something, too
and not only chop down and harvest

vulnerability is a lot of things
it's to lie under the tattoo-knife
to show openness toward the world
to be naked in front of others

to let your true self reveal
to let your true name be heard
to navigate below the stars
much the same way your foremothers
went through life and measure it
through the lenses of "how many hearts
they did touch during their whole life-span?"
what markings did you put on earth?
what tunes did you put down wearily?
what ink-stains and stories were told?
how many seeds of life did you plant?
what did the ships you sailed carry?

Foremothers

Sometimes the thoughts go deep at night
Lili Elbe, Christine Jorgensen
Saga Becker, Caroline Cossey
Marsha Pay it no mind Johnson
Frances Thompson, Aleksa Lundberg
and other women throughout history
who plowed the fields and cleared the roads
to the rooms that I linger in
That I am on my way to crash into

my foremothers, so to speak

and if I'm completely honest
I probably think about them more
than my own grandmothers
paternal, and maternal too
an ego child, void of history?
or was the axis Stockholm-Värmland
too big to ever bridge
through new books and internet
Danish Girl and other movie-pieces
at least it's easier to talk about
but if they would have lived today
would they say my One True Name?

some ships meet in silent nights
some just pass by one another
in the waves of the Vänern-lake

the South Pacific or the Caribbean

but then Polynesia opens!
fakaleiti, fa'afafine
akava'ine, moe aikane
and *māhū* smashing up a hole
in the gilded cage of flesh
that being trans means to me

we are the strangest fucking culture
throughout all of history
when it comes to the gender-norms
and the Lutheran work ethics

(can't recall my grandpa ever
speaking in extended sentences
to me or even ask that much
before I passed my driver's test
and began
studying to be a journalist)
and sure, blood is thick but water
Polynesia has *a lot* of that

Congo-Chicago-Stockholm

Ancient men traded cattle
Before Columbus was lost in travel, ancient canoes got paddled
Before the horse saddle there was camel
Spears before arrow, arrow before ammo
Tribal paint before camo-
Flage, chief before sarge, or lieutenant
Village elders before the Senate
Used to sail the seas before the compass was invented
Ancient people spoke free, they didn't need a first Amendment
In the beginning, the drum was the text sendin'
There was moons before months, and time before minutes

– Nasir Jones

what do we Europeans
so called sea-faring people
Hellenes, Swedes, Istrians
Iberians, Brits, Celts and Geats
Danes, Etruscians, Phoenicians, Romans
about sailing longer water-stretches
than our fantasy allows us to

hic sunt dracones or here be dragons
sat on maps for quite a while
 "white stains" on the White Man's maps
for too long the rule of thumb
was "point to random area"
maybe put a flag in there
name it after your family

your title or your Christian name
your daughters or your mistresses
so, all of a sudden: Queen Maud's land
smack-bang in the harsh cold Antarctica
and imagine the imaginativeness
leaving Portsmouth just to arrive in
Portsmouth
England becoming New England
South Wales becoming New South Wales

"New" Caledonia

during our crude Migration Period
when us Europeans beat each other bloody
in tribal wars and enmities
the Polynesians would sail away
in what we label as medieval
cultures built so well-made boats
canoes that would take them from
Fiji and Melanesia
to Easter Island and Hawaii
in an axis– imagine this–
corresponding to the measurements
of Stockholm-Chicago-Congo
the Pacific is a vast ocean
and it doesn't stay that still, either
but hosts and boasts such vast stretches
that the concept of distances melt
when a ship reaches Point Nemo
nestled in the South Pacific
it would be 2,700
kilometers from nearest land-mass

I've heard that at a certain point in time
the closest human beings would
be found at the international space station
416 kilometers up

what do we Europeans
so called sea-faring people
Hellenes, Swedes, Istrians
Iberians, Brits, Celts and Geats
Danes, Etruscians, Phoenicians, Romans
about sailing longer water-stretches
than our fantasy allows us to

I live in a town with several harbors,
I've never even
stepped unto a boat in Malmö
and I think I fear *Stora Havet*
that Jakob Hellman came close to grasping
but never really understood

sand-atoms in Sahara, drops of H2O
in enormous watery containers
without walls, really, to hold them down
except gravity and those we've built
I think I want to perceive it like that
even if openness frightens me
how we meet in one single ocean
in threads of life-energy
I remember Söderbysjön
a lake nestled in southern Stockholm
it made me feel exactly this

Forest vs death (on knockout)

These forests carry everything
because in some ways, the forest is me
in little threads of common atoms
thoughts only separating them

When I swim the first stroke I find
my anxiety swallowed by the water
and I'm sent through the traumas back
to childhood simplicity

The loops go in circles here
and I believe in *instant karma*
I lock eyes with a water-snake
and I gently let it pass by me

The Doula of Death wanted to talk to me
remind me of all black, sad death
I just smiled much like Mona Lisa
said, look, at the soft clear sunrise

I thought it was a gargantuan task
to chase away the shadows cowering
to kill the darkness with the light
but the morning mist just a-rolled on in

I stood in a gathering of life
I was soil and rock and earth
I was nothing really, only stardust
that solved the mysteries of life for me

Budget of infinite light

Oh, to be a wasteress
Big-pocket Arvida out of All the World
oh, I would sprinkle little stars!
into the hearts of all mankind
create weaves with beautiful
patterns stunning in their beauty
because, as Irving Layton said
death is a name for beauty not in use

As the One High Priestess, Elected Queen
I'd create a two-state solution
Palestine for the Palestinians
and no apartheid-settler nonsense
peace in all of Middle East
dethrone the false Saudi prophets
the proxy states of the ayatollah
give Fatima Mohammed's roll
peace to North Macedonia

prosperity to Tajikistan
success to the Kyrgyz people
fill Amu Darja to the brim
make Turkmenistan, Uzbekistan
flowering meadow-bed
Lands of Milk and Wild Wild Honey

I'd protect Polynesia
unmake all the nuclear tests

on the atolls outside Bikini
I'd fill the craters under Kazakhstan
I'd write a budget out of Light
I'd be a harsh but fair heavenly priestess
light stars in every one of us

Good morning Fiji

August night at Limhamns andelshamn 2023

Pro Primo: the trans flag-shimmering
orange yellow mystery
an event of the firmament
the canopy glowing embossed
and you have no problem imagining
why some humans looked at the heavenly light
and called it (for lack of a better word)
God, or Ra, or Amaterasu

but that is just the
overture
pro segundo, we proceed: crescendo
as the contents of the Sun condenses
into a red, shimmering, dazey haze
quite short and quite memorable
you get the icing of the Very Cake:

Red lights
over the wind spinners
flaming red over in Copenhagen
everything is for free, elevated, and you get

The barge haulers at the Volga-river

The primeval forces of Spindletop
Baku-flames out of Bessarabia

Tierra del Fuego tears of teal
and the Melanesian mightiness

all inside a single sunset
where everything is one and all.

Ere the red Sun rises!
Spectral type G2V, smack-bang-bullseye, Milky Way
4,6 billion years young
15 million-degrees-Celsius-hot
looking much like a million bucks
absolute magnitude (M V {\displaystyle M_{V}} Mv 4,83)
Helios, the Giver of Life on Earth

and somewhere else, a place that is not
Limhamn's harbour where the rich folks live
just stroked and caressed by the heavenly body
who (in a non-binary yet binary way) promises
its very soon *auf wiedersehn*
and the Sun takes shine on newer places
whose names are not Malmö, Sweden
they maybe carry
names even more beautiful:

Nuku'alofa and Nasilai
Koumac, Port Vela and Nouméa
Bikenibeu and Cristobal
Longana, Luganville, Lenakel
Rakiraki, Vandravandra

Yangganga, Naweni, Savusavu
Lautoka, Ba, Nadi and Suva
Sigatoka and Nalele

A new August aspires there
a Day we have just abandoned
and soon will be light candles for
but the promise lies much in the open
in the great and stormy Pacific Ocean
I just want to take all of this
write From Sweden with Love on the envelope
hope to see you soon, Southern Seas

Good morning, Fiji!
we give you the sun
keep it, use it, live with it
and let's get 50/50 custody!

Polynesian storm

Natten är här och alla katter är grå
men i den svartaste timmen, min vän
finns så mycket att lära, då är gryningen nära
då ska dagen snart randas igen

Tiden är sen och jag slår upp mina blå
mot hela rymden och vad ser jag i den?
jo, att allt indirekt i universum är släkt
vi är stoft av en stjärna, min vän

– Ola Magnell

Your existence matters. Take heart. We need you here.

– Facebook-group To Write Love on Her Arms

I. Warmth collides with coolness

Are we born not knowing, are we born knowing all?
Are we growing wiser, or are we just growing tall?
Can you read thoughts, can you read palms?
Can you predict the future, can you see storms... coming?

– Damian Marley

a shaking of the world's foundation
do you know how storms are born?
first, heat-masses generate
then coldness vomits out its outroar
gives birth to a new El Niño
an angry child crying out revenge

it's been boiling for so long now
almost burnt the beans inside the pot
it's been cooking for generations
in small spots under the surfacing atolls

but it ain't *haggis*,
it's not *kæstur hákarl*
it beats croc-pot and pulled-pork-cookings
and barbeque-marinatings
a thread through days:
colored clouds (of flurried insights)
a murder of mystery crows
sometimes it's hard to hold unto
something solid in the stream of thoughts

warmth collides with cool, cool windstreams
we hurt because we have been hurt
cools down when you let it boil
warms up when we should let it cool

we think of breadfruits for the Caribbean
not of the actual Caribbean

imagine a dream-vision-Tahiti
we don't see Tahiti proper

then we think "fucking Monsanto/Exxon"
not "we're doing what we've always done"
then we think "oh, funny-looking outfits"
as if the Samis were some copy-cats
and not
the goddamn
original

colonialism lives and breathes
from Sápmi to the Caribbean
the Antilles to Bougainville
in you, in me, in all our thoughts
and if tears would help at all
I'd fill the Pacific Ocean
if I could help it by disappearing
I'd be gone tomorrow morning

but it's not that simple, really

storms are like us, I think
foaming with righteous rage
strikes like the Walkürenritt
roars like the lion of Judah
barks like a Cerberus
with heads of hate and greed and power
become the wolf we feed the most

then comes a much more peaceful time
it cools down, it makes amends
goes on world tours of forgiveness
in the form of some still, quiet breezes
as if to say "keep loving me
even if I tend to tear it down
the things we have built together"

as if to say "keep loving me
even though I am so hopeless
I've got warm winds inside of me
and they are still as a calm lagoon
they soothe like coconut milk and water
they echo like the caves of old
below Makatea in the summer"

but the sun has got stains, too
doing things much too hastily
not until Maui's lasso
choke-holds it and puts pressure on it
it sees the point and slows things down
catching its breath after a working-week

maybe grabs a cold *otai*
or a *kava* to smooth things down
after a feast with *umukai*
asking itself between the bites
moans to the stars and to the moon:
I am playing the part of Sun ok?

And stars, as all of you know
you lunatics who've asked the moon
quietly seen the star signs glisten
they can point out directions sometimes
but seldom gives plain, straight-up answers

but the Pole Star that the Polynesians
for centuries has gazed upon
gives the Sun at least a partial answer
says: you're doing the best you can
and sometimes, ashes make the best of soil
and storms can clean up anything

II. Blackbird in mi'kmaq

Ever since my awkward attempt at assimilation into suburbia, I have longed to return, however symbolically, to the harmonious place of my childhood where everyone belonged and played happily together (or so I remembered).

- Miriam Kahn, Tahiti Beyond the Postcard

You know what social media-streams are like!
much like the Pacific Ocean
on a windy day whipped by hurricanes
in million little teacup-storms
but usually, something sticks

2019
International Year of Indigenous Languages
did you that? I know I didn't
and in Nova Scotia
Eskasoni, Cape Breton
Allison Bernard Memorial
High School a clip was recorded
a young woman accompanied by
a number of men with brand-guitars
singing Blackbird like a goddess would
in mi'kmaq that spoke like spring-time
and it's no mere "must watch-video"
anthropological exposé
it is to keep and preserve worlds
the seeing and the perception

language is such a part in that
and I find it very important

I don't compare myself with
a language nearly eradicated
but just speaking of the matter
memories, language and tribes

I possessed no written language
or spoken language of trans when I was young
a dangerous curiosity
an animal drift, a strangeness, sickness
that is how I interpreted it
and this was the 1990's
what a closeted Spice Girl-world it was
even if we still had the Beatles
Blackbird singing in the dead of night

Languages are our placeholders
pain has worlds that's all its own
actions, ponderings and place
every language has a unique pain
and worthy sentimentality
humor, richness, ways to view the world
monoculture can seem beautiful
like the rape-seed fields in Scania
but for a long, sustainable continuity
agricultural husbandry to last out ages
it takes many different views
a lot of languages, its weight of years

because only the grey of asphalt
remains if we only have one language

but don't falter, don't lose your hope
one soul is all it takes to keep
the language
dancing
singing,
vibrating!
and all of the dandelion-seeds
are the plants that will grow to crush
the stupidity of brutalism
the rusty, leaking Empire
and populate it with vibrating life
sing Blackbird in mi'kmaq
like a goddess resonating

I read the news today, oh boy
most of them are probably gone tomorrow
but Blackbird in mi'kmaq stuck

III. The World Wind/That Final Poem

I did not emerge
From my hospital bed, half-goddess
a Valar of Tolkien's Arda
claiming what mortal shell I will
but I emerged from the fog of war
of XGEVA and cushions of morphine
with new titanium and bone-cement
and with color, form and contours
infinitely closer to myself

the first thing I tried on was a bra
a rivulet of calm along my spine
so the first thing I went out to buy
was panties, burning my underpants
and in the bliss of that summer – 2019, I was in love
in the self that I was beckoning
until the healthcare line ruined everything

if you're not feeling holy
which you tend to do, from time to time
(And if you don't, girl, boy, gender-fluid *leaning in*
You are a walking, talking fucking deity!)
you feel most pre-makeover
subhuman, orcish, Frankenstein
conjugated scrap-on body parts
barely making fleshly connection
breasts that have been cut in half
your scrotum: something hideous
and it's a full-time job to feel sexy

when you mourn your physical body
every morning hating bath-room mirrors
as though it were made in Mordor
and only there can be destroyed

Morgoth sang a dissonance
in the song of Ainulindalë
that cacophony cuts through all of me
with all the strength of the Patriarchy

It oozes with raw ambition
that sound, and the selfishness
form cold, damp dark territories
sharp cliffs carved out inside of me
a Gorgoroth-plain of power-hungry enemies
watchful peace with a slow cat's sharpened teeth
playing with a bunch of field mice

and they cry
benplockerska, benplockerska
cishet-winds cry "bone pickeress"
at me from a cold Parnassus
benplockerska, benplockerska
disturber of the smoky peace
runner-up, parvenu, *riche nouveau*
in the haze of patriarchy
second and third wave feminists
still alive, eagerly craving fights
losing their sniper-rifle-scopes
in the fog of their privileges
they shout *benplockerska, benplockerska*

as if I were a mere intruder
a rat amongst the kitchen-maids
sent out to poison the winter rations
of the apples-of-Eden harvest
with forked, yellow teeth of Man
preparing poison like a spitting cobra
behind my shy trans-woman smile
decoy, ready to finally launch attacks
to strike at the heart of womanhood

it's the gruesome and exclusionary
idea and thought that I went in through
the back-door of womanhood
a shortcut
to the Garden's apples
not deserving any type of grace
that turns the Virginia Woolf
tap of gas on slowly, slowly
perforating Xanax-large
holes in my head sometime

you can
never be a woman
you will
never be a mother
you can't ever
hope to be normal
you will never
be one of us
you are tainted
with the germ called Man

you will always
be your gender

and when the curtain fell down:
I don't want to be somebody's "parent"
don't want to be some sweet soul's "father"
for me, the only option is
to be someone's
Mamma (Mother)
and this, people in Cis-country
it is crucial that you understand this
even if everything else passes
to not be able
to become pregnant
not even have the
possibility
it is a sorrow piercing dreams and fears

I have to realize, to myself
that it is a great sorrow
how it is a grand sorrow
sort my body out
dock ports with the mothership
be recognized as a subsidiary
in the concern of Womanhood™
be accepted by the stockholders
the gatekeepers of woman-stock
then I can begin to breathe

then we can start talking

and thanks to a certain Irish clinic (and finally Swedish
healthcare)
that conversation is well underway

and

That is only a shell of me
the remains that are man in me
my yellowed, dried-out last year's grass
ready for desert winds and new-born fires
beautiful like a frozen insect
in some stale herbarium
and with enough stunning beauty
posing for the onlooking women

and my forlorn years of youth

I can't go around regretting them
I can't go and add a dead-name blues
to every tune I ever chant
I wouldn't, couldn't live like this
but maybe, at the speech therapist
my voice can be made feminine
so that I can join my fellow sisters
(Pol Pot and all red-flag wavers
their song echoing through creation
praising storms that must come at last
can't be a part of this choir
obviously)

naked before the eyes

of the women taking pottery classes
full focus, nothing sexual
Åke Hans, Bredgatan 5
where Strindberg used to go to drink
with Emil Kléen, his closeted friend
with whom he just might have had a love affair

for structure and stability
the silence breaks now and then
when clay is slabbed unto a work-bench
the needles are for staging up
a stale masculine clay-figure
but it's an effigy, it isn't me
that's someone else there taking form
about to become Prometheus
but still, pretty macabre, right?
a pin right down through my head

one night in life
– and just like that –
A lightning bolt hit me,
felt just like that
thing I hear they call *satori*

the storm took me through windy seas
of evil, seesaw, dead-wind waves
a language I did not master
inhabiting a deflated dinghy,
my sicknesses, diagnoses
the size of tall ocean liners

but the only one in black and white
was a giant cell tumor growing
so the beginning of my 2019
were some doses of XGEVA
and some trips to the hospital
with crutches and a will to fight
but Panchamama! I was tired then

but the pro's at the hospital
new and shiny in the north of Lund
(where Emil Kléen once died at 30)
in the heart of the Central Block
a seventies Barad-dûr tower
but after months of medicine
the doctors carved up my leg
and replaced the dead tissue there
with titanium and bone cement
just south of my left kneecap
and through morphine and massive pain
catheter on my bodily sex
(gender?) I'd just come home
less than a week post-op
someone driving scalpels into my body
the sickness
of the morphine rush
sank away
and was replaced
by the strongest feeling
I've ever ever felt, I think.

It rose like a summery *fata morgana*

mist shrouding a calm lagoon
palms swaying in harmony
a sort of holy *hajj*, Kailash
Damaskus-light or Sermon on the mount
clear streams ran into my blood
my brain pieced everything together
the Ariadne-thread shimmering

That Feeling was the Transfeeling

and it had reared its beautiful face to me
through guilt and shame and shadow-work
sickening resistances
my machinery was losing screws
I'd think of Stalingrad on a summer's day
in the middle of a quiet moment
sitting with girlfriends and one-night stands
boy, how I've hated the hetero-norm
and I've slithered, rattled, like a rattlesnake
to make myself fit into it
I'd take it out on myself
and others in my surroundings
never physical, ever spiritual

but no more of that old grain
for the one awaiting growing seeds
happens to be me these days

I've found my flame imperishable
I'm Embla, not Ask this life
Eve, not Adam-san

Narai I am, and no Maono
that is the true shape of my heart
Caribbean winds took me there
and soon maybe Polynesian storms
will shake up some heavy floods
but I find peace in my paddling
I will reach for a safer harbor

and when I see the pins and needles
they pin into their clay-class-voodoo's
the little golems made of me
for structure and stability
receiving life in life-less ovens
remaining forever effigies
but all of that, see, that's not me
that is not the "me" I see
and I don't know about other storms
but I believe in Polynesia
I believe in my fellow siblings
my soulmates with commons goals
in the name of love, we're mutineers
jumping off the ocean liners
returning to the still-warm sea
in love and peaceful harmony
I believe that after heavy storms
comes the calm breath of a new morning
times of blossoming after forest fires
Caribbean winds mixing in
to something I call the great World Wind.

you know, on those summer nights

when the winds are one big family
and all connected through the soil
that feeling that we have named June
that feeling that we have named Love
all that remains my manifesto
and we will work out all the rest

Caribbean sea
to the South Pacific
Northern Sápmi to
Abya Yala
like a rainbow coming after rain
like queers after the hetero-norm
like women after all the men
indigenous people on some post-Caucasian-shit

one love to all,
Arvida out

It was still dark when the wind died down, and Tehina had to use the paddle. She noticed that the backwash swelled, and rose to a miti vatau, one of those echoes of some remote but heavy storm. She found comfort in the notion that swells like that often die down as soon as they arise.

– Sverre Holmsen, Sjungande korall (Singing coral).

Outroduction

Here, in a *miti vatau,* a vague echo of a heavier storm, ends
the tale of Arvida, the Caribbean, Polynesia and the world.
For now. At least it felt like an ending when I wrote the final
stanzas in Swedish (they heal me everytime I read them), in
a warm attic-room in Malmö in May 2021. But a few things
have happened since then, if you know what I mean? It is
not possible (without starting a new book) to summarize all
of the world-turning events, but the covid bleeding into a
full-scale aggression war by a dictatorship (the Russian
Federation) on a democracy (Ukraine), coloring European
soil with its old-time favourite feed: human blood. That
could be a start. A right-wing-swing in Swedish politics
placed the most conservative government since the 1930's
(with a "budget out of the 30-years war [1618-1648]", as a
Swedish journalist put it), backed by neo-nazis in power,
could be a continuation. The US election turning into a
hostile takeover still unfolding, with fascist key signatures
such as extreme violence (storming into workplaces, schools
and even reservations claiming BIPOC and Native
Americans are not "real" and "legal" Americans), targeting
minorities and using vile language and ugly gestures,
complete with the actual Nazi salute (Elon Musk, Steve
Bannon). At the same time, in foreign politics, the United
States of America, now de facto in the UN, forms an axis of
evil, together with Russia and North Korea. Not exactly a
democratic dream-team. All of this makes me think dark
thoughts like "the Thanksgiving Natives should have given
the Europeans the treatment that the people of North

Sentinel gave John Alleu Chau – a vest full of arrows to the chest", amongst *many* other things.

What can I say that I haven't already said in about 170 pages? It is crucial to resist these people, for they do not love us. Not any of us. Only themselves. Resist in every possible way.

And I can say that a purchase of this book (thanks for shopping!), will support not only me but organizations protecting transgender-, Native- and BIPOC-minorities, in the US and the world.

Let us end on another note. *No, let's not talk of love or change/ and things we can't untie/ your eyes are soft with sorrow/ hey, that's no way to say goodbye* as the muse from Montreal (one L. Cohen) wrote and sang.

I am so glad that I found my way at such a relatively early age in life. I am so glad that I was accepted by my friends and family. I am so proud of all my siblings in transness and queerness all around the world, who live on Earth now or only live in memories, you are all so beautiful. I am so honored to be a (ever so small) part of the struggles against racism, ableism, transphobia, homophobia, predatory behaviour against fellow human beings, plants, animals and nature, against unjust conditions, whether it's class-related, minority-related or any other group of people suffering at the hands of others.

I am so thankful to She Rises Studios for believing in me.

And I am so hopeful that something better will come out of all this darkness.

I hope this book has changed your life, ever so slightly. Because it changed mine.

Now, let's change the world.

Talk to me on Facebook:
https://www.facebook.com/profile.php?id=100092459993992

Talk to me on Instagram:
https://www.instagram.com/arvidasvenskeauthor/

Talk to me on Bluesky:
https://bsky.app/profile/arvidasvenske.bsky.social

Listen to my podcast Cohenpodden

Thank you for reading this, and for being you!

With the warmth of the sun itself,

Arvida Juni Svenske

Explain yourself!

Gladly. Here is a word list of almost all of the words, concepts and phrases that occur in other languages than English (as well as introductions to writers, poems and songwriters) starting from the beginning.

p.3 Édouard Glissant was a writer, poet, philosopher, and literary critic from Martinique. A very good one, from what I've read. Belonging to the same school of thought (and actual school, Lycée Schœlcher in Martinique) as Aimé Césaire, Léon Damas, Léopold Senghor and Frantz Fanon, one of black consciousness. This quote is from the harrowing 1956 poem collection *Les Indes* (in English 1992, *The Indies*, trans. Dominique O'Neill), which in the Swedish translation by Magdalena Sørensen & Catherine Delpech-Hellsten read *Indiorna: en dikt om den nakna nattens erövrare* (a poem of the conquerors of the naked night). You will never recover from reading it, in fact I hope that you read it and that you don't.

p.3-5 "I'm an American, our names don't mean shit", says Bruce Willis's character (Butch) in Quentin Tarantino's Pulp Fiction, after being asked what his name means by a taxi driver named Esmeralda Villalobos (roughly Emerald Wolftown!).

Oh but they do. To sum all the names on the first pages up: Stacy Ann Ferguson (Fergie) might be familiar to the average reader, as well as the late, great Mohammed Ali. Panchamama is the Mother Goddess of the Kuna-people, encompassing and at the same time being the world. According to some myths, as I understand it, we walk on her body. Abya Yala ("earth in full blossom" or "land in its full maturity") was the name for South America before the Europeans named it, much like Alkebulan was the name for Africa. You know, we're not even sure about how the name "America" came into place. Amerigo Vespucci is the go-to-guy, but there are some other theories, such as the one regarding Richard ap Meryk (Amerike), an Anglo-Welsh merchant, royal customs officer and sheriff of Bristol. In 1497, he supposedly sponsored one of the first British ships to cross the Atlantic, according to this theory. Pretty debunked, as I understand it. But you've also got the theory of America stemming from a Nicaraguan mountain, the Amerrisque, and that this was what was relayed to Columbus and his crew. One Augustus Le Plongeon suggested in 1875 that "The name AMERICA or AMERRIQUE in the Mayan language means, a country of perpetually strong wind, or the Land of the Wind, and ... the [suffixes] can mean ... a spirit that breathes, life itself".

But you know, and I know, that it's true name is Turtle Island.

p.3. *Blut und Boden* means blood and soil, a Nazi slogan expressing Nazi Germany's ideal of a racially defined national body ("Blood") united with a settlement area ("Soil").

p.4 *det stör mig när jag arbetar* means "it bothers me while I work" and was coined by Nino Mick, a Swedish poet/train driver in their beautiful and painful 2018 book *Tjugofemtusen kilometer nervtrådar* (Twenty five thousand kilometers of nerve-ends).

p.5 Sykes-Picot, after the British Christian straight white man sir Mark Sykes (Boer-war veteran, i.e. war-criminal) and the French Christian straight white man François Georges-Picot. Together with the Russian Christian straight white man Sergej Dimitrijevitj Sazonov they negotiated the secret deal that basically fucks the Middle East up to this day.

James Cook, Samuel Wallis and Louis Antoine Bougainville were three Christian straight white men who went to sea, drew maps and convinced themselves and the world they "discovered" things and therefore named them. In Cook's case, the Cook Islands, in Wallis's case Wallis (of the Wallis & Futuna) and in Bougainvilles case a beautiful flower (bougainvillea, a favorite of Paul Simon's along with the Rose of Jericho) and a beautiful island (Bougainville) which should have beautiful support for a beautiful independence from Papua New Guinea.

p.7 Cortez, known as Hernán Cortés during his life-time, was a poster-boy for one of the worst movements in the world: the crazed, perverted takeover of Abya Yala by Christian fundamentalists. May he not exactly rest in peace.

p.8 Sveaskog is Sweden's largest, state-owned foresting company. They seem hell-bent on making a profit off the Sami-people's (indigenous to Sápmi, an area encompassing the north of Sweden, Norway, Finland and a slice of Russia) land and to take Bientije, Lill-Skarje, Gihmiesgielas, Guossavare, Biellovare and other Sami places from the actual owners, continuing a long, Swedish tradition of killing, plundering and christening the Sami people by force. Yes, we still do that shit too. But we are mere Salieris to the Mozart of indigenous genocides: the United States of America.

p.12 *Skogsrå* is a Nordic, mythological creature. Basically, the front of her is a beautiful, naked (!) woman, and with it, she used to lure men into the woods. But her back is a hollow tree trunk, and when you see it, it's too late. You're ensnared by her. Either to be eaten, to be her slave or to wander in the woods until you die of hunger and thirst. In this case, it refers to the subhumanness you sometimes experience as a transwoman in a transphobic world. Fake it til' you make it, but beneath it all you're just some… creature in the woods.

p.15 *them bones are gonna rise again* is from an old spiritual, a song that tells the story of the expulsion of Adam and Eve from the Garden of Eden, but also metaphorically describes the return of and survival of Black slaves.

Claudio Magris in *Non luogo a procedere* (Blameless) also draws parallels between the black slaves and the Jewish survivors of WW2:

But quite alike, actually. The black slave who escapes from the plantation, up amongst the hills, knowing that he will get caught, defiantly leaving traces in the high grass on the hills. As we all know, he will die, but he does not give up; after him, thanks to him, there will be other slaves, other rebels, that no extermination can exterminate. When Aron Lieukant was put on the train to Auschwitz he sent a message to his children Berta and Simon: "Don't drink ice-cold beverages when you're sweating in the summer". And those idiots in brown shirts and swastikas thought they could destroy such people? Faced with Mr. Lieukant's message even La Risiera is a petty little hole. If I had that message, I'd superimpose it so it would dominate the entire museum. In fact, that message and a chain ripped apart by a black slave could make up the entire museum. No more shall they in bondage toil, let my people free. Millions of dead; they, we, me and mine and the me and mines of my mines, but these bones will be resurrected, *dese bones gwine rise again*, not just bones but flesh and blood, bodies made to love. It's not for nothing the poor Pharaohs and their minions fear the power of the Black and the Jewish genitalia.

p.*16 Antillergulden*, the Dutch currency on "their" Caribbean islands.

p.17 I was going to call this poem "There's a smile in every Hershey" (much of the sugar used by them before Castro derived from Cuba). But nah.

p.18 White Man's Burden is an 1800's-poem by Rudyard Kipling – and a rap album released in 2006 by the Swedish rapper Promoe out of Looptroop Rockers. The definitions of this "burden" differ, so to speak. Kipling means that the "white Man" has a burden, and it is to enslave and thereby "civilize" other "races", Promoe means that the white man's burden is having to live with people thinking and acting like Kipling. Listen to the latter, heed not the first.

p.19 Iron Curtain – coined by Winston Churchill, the name for the division between the Communist East and the Democratic West in Europe During the Cold War. The Soviets and the East Germans called the Berlin Wall, about a hundred miles of divisive concrete right through Berlin, the Anti-Fascist Protection Wall.

The Aral Sea was once one of the greatest lakes of the earth, sucked dry by the Soviets wanting to be self-sufficient in the produce of cotton. They *almost* succeeded (drill baby drill!) but in return killed an *entire ecosystem of an inner-sea*. It is now divided between Kazakhstan (where it shows signs of recovering) and Uzbekistan (where a desert with poison salts has taken its place). If you want to pin a name of blame to this crime, make it Sharof Rashidov. He ran the Uzbek SSR with an iron-fist until his death in 1983, reporting ever higher production, manipulating and exaggerating the numbers so that Moscow demanded even more cotton. Kind of like, you know, market-capitalism.

Las Mariposas, "the butterflies", the Mirabal sisters, were executed in 1960 and became a symbol of resistance against the dictatorship of Rafael Trujillo in the Dominican Republic.

p.22 Khéya Wíta, the Lakota name for Turtle Island (the American continent).

como una mariposa, una abeja – like a butterfly, like a bee.

p.23 Estados Unidos – United States. In fact, *estadounidense*, not americano, is more commonly used in Mexico. Because united-staters are not the only Americans. The Apple TV-series *Acapulco* tells this well.

p.24 The poem June gloom (junidimma in Swedish) contains extrapolations of a Swedish rendition originally published in my Swedish poetry collection *Ovinter*. It is inspired by Paul Simon's little masterpiece Think too much (b) (vastly superior to Think too much (a)).

Det är som om allt jag sagt och gjort
Samlas i Los Angeles
Till tiden då vi var där
Mitt uppe i kärleksstress

Sen är det som att iakttas
Av någon högre makt
De släcker sakta skissborden
Känslan förbleknar snabbt

It's as if everything I've said and done
gathers in Los Angeles
to the time when we were there
tangled up in the stress of love

Then it is as if I'm being watched
by some higher power
they shut the lights under the plane table
the feeling fades away

Det sägs att hjärnans vänstra del
Håller den högra i ett schack
Och den högra, den hålls vaken
Genom varje drömlös natt

En kväll kom månljus in till mig
Gardinen hade hål
Det sa "det som varit är förbi
och snart är vintern vår"

They say the left side of the brain
it dominates the right like in a chess-game
and the right side, it's being held awake
through every dreamless night

One night, moonlight came to me
the curtain had a hole
it said "what has been has already passed
and soon winter will be spring"

Det är säkert övertänk

means maybe I think too much.

grabbatös is a word used in Skåne (Scania, a region in the south of Sweden where Malmö is located) meaning "boygirl".

p.35 Central Asia came into my life through studies at the university, then deepened through cooperation with the Swedish organization Centralasiengrupperna (Central Asia Groups) and the Kyrgyz feminist organization Novi Ritm (New Rhythm). I was supposed to go there, but contracted complications from the tumor which occurs in the final poem, and so I had to cancel it. I love, cherish and root so much for this part of the world, torn between Russia, China and all the other superpowers of the world but with fantastic landscapes and cultures. Erika Fatland has written one of the best books I've ever read about this (and best book in all categories): *Sovietistan*. Read that, along with her trailblazer *The Border: A Journey Around Russia Through North Korea, China, Mongolia, Kazakhstan, Azerbaijan, Georgia, Ukraine, Belarus, Lithuania, Poland, Finland, Norway, and the Northeast Passage* and new worlds will open up to you.

Jamilia and Daniar was a sort of Romeo and Juliet-story I heard about, a powerful love story in a culture where arranged marriages are the norm.

p.41 Jogorku Kenesh is the Kyrgyz parliament, *ak-kalpak* is a traditional Kyrgyz hat worn by men. Bishkek is the Kyrgyz capital, *alu kachuu* is the name for the (still going strong, unfortunately) not-so-proud tradition of "bride kidnapping", or "girl kidnapping" as it should be called.

p.45 *Sonderweg* is often used of Germany, to describe the process of why German history differed so much from its European neighbours. Here, I apply it to Russia.

p.53 *Folkets hus*, in Swedish literally "The People's House", is historically associated with organizations affiliated with the Swedish labour movement. The idea is that culture in different forms should belong to everybody without having to pay a fortune. Folkets park ("the people's park") is a prevalent feature of many Swedish towns. These places mean a lot to Swedes and hold fond memories.

rus means intoxication.

p.54 *han, hon, hen* (he, she, they), Swedish pronouns.

p.59 *du jour* – sort of a French word for the "current trend", something "popular, fashionable, or prominent at a particular time" as Merriam-Webster puts it.

The Slovenian and Greek episodes are true stories. In Slovenian, women means *ženska* and man *človek*, so the ž and the č didn't help much. And I can't read Greek, unfortunately. The closest I've come was one course in

189

Bulgarian history, but the cyrillic letters never nestled in my brain.

p.64 To hear the soothing bluesy timbre of Barbro Hörberg (ripped away from us way too soon, – by the old scourge of breast-cancer – at the age of 43), a Mary Oliver of a Swedish singer-songwriter, is almost like watching some old black and white Armenian movie. You have to meditate yourself into the state where you are susceptible to the nuances. Our modern brains are too sugar-rushed, color-coated and fast-paced to fully understand the melancholy. But I recommend you to try. In songs such as the self-explanatory *Gråt i gräset* (Crying in the grass), *Störst av allt är rädslan* (Fear is the greatest of all), *November min vän* (November my friend), *Vill du bli min soptipp* (Do you want to be my rubbish dump) and *Jag älskar en kille som ingen annan tycker om* (I love a guy that nobody else likes) as well as the lovely *Gamla älskade barn* (Old beloved child) dedicated to an old drunkard sleeping on a park-bench covers up pretty much all of the spectrum of *vardagskänslor* (everyday feelings), emotions that perhaps some would deem "petty", but in fact, is *life itself*. And her masterpiece is the album and the song *Med ögon känsliga för grönt* (With eyes sensitive to green), which could be the Swedish national anthem. I mean, what else do you need in life than:

Det regnade men bilderna blev bra
Det var ett egendomligt ljus den dan
Vi fyllde våra ögon
Med ljuset och tankarna på allt det nya

Och tänk i parken
Om våren
Med ögon känsliga för grönt
Och kastanjeblad som paraplyer
Jag älskade dej då, det gör jag nu

It rained, but the pictures turned out good
it was a strange light that day
we filled our eyes
with the light and the thoughts of all the new
and imagine the park
in spring
with eyes sensitive to green
with leaves of chestnuts for umbrellas
I loved you then, and I still do

Never have I ever felt this song to my core as when a) I
discovered other colors in life as I started to transition b)
when we landed at Arlanda in Stockholm after three days at
a Canadian airport, overlooking only the tarmac and a
doomsday sky of gray matter after a hurried flight from a
situation I found myself in (that story is outside the scope of
this book). *My green homeland,* I felt as I saw the pine-trees,
the fir-trees standing tall, the other greenery starting to
blossom in mid-April. *Det var ett egendomligt ljus den dagen.*
I'll drink an alcohol-free beverage (seven years sober!) to that
feeling.

p.67 Åke Hans was an old tavern in the beautiful town of
Lund (Grove) in Skåne, close to Malmö. Now it belongs to an

organization called Folkuniversitetet (People's university), providing classes in (among many other things) clay-pottery. I was a nude model there a couple of times. August Strindberg is one of Sweden's greatest writers, revered and hated, known for his social democratic, radical and anti-bureaucratic views (and sadly for his misogyny and conservative views on marriage). Some, including myself depending on the day, believe he was actually bisexual or maybe even gay. The closest thing we come to confirming this is preserved letters, writings on the topic, attending a so-called *Tuntenball* (sort of a queer ballroom-event) in Berlin, and his relationship with the Lund-poet Emil Kléen. However, this is not confirmed as fact – and probably never will be. *The past is a foreign country; they do things differently there*, as L.P. Hartley wrote.

Adam and Eve is a Judeo-Christian myth about (heterosexual) love marking out the symbolic roles of men and women.

Embla and Ask is a Nordic myth about the first two humans on earth, of (heterosexual) love marking the symbolic union between men and women.

Narai and Maono is a Polynesian myth of (heterosexual) love marking the symbolic union between men and women.

p.74 Page 28 is a book-store and a culture scene in Malmö, founded by Lou Mattei in 2019 after visiting *Les mots à la bouche*, an lgbtqia+2-bookshop in Paris. Page 28 comes from the movie *Portrait of a woman on fire*, but I won't spoil that beautiful, emotional gale-storm of a movie for you if you haven't seen it yet.

p.77-78 The title-poem of this entire entity of words is quite self-explanatory, but it deserves to mention how much this poem (the living of it, the making of it and the readings in Swedish of it) changed my life. A lot, you guys, a lot. The dress in question was a pink, silky thing that I bought on my "summer-of-love" in 2019, I still have it in the closet and if my estimations are correct, it still fits (but that's a big if). I cannot stress enough how much therapy has helped in this process, poetry/arts/craft alone is *not* enough to process things like this. Probably, everything mentioned in this poem might have actually saved my life. Thank you to all the human beings helping me along this journey. And know this, if you struggle: you are *never* alone.

p.80 All of the historical figures mentioned in this poem are either explained earlier in this stack-of-many-words or might be common knowledge (but also, no shame if they do not ring any bells to you!). But the life and work of Alberto Fujimori, Japanese-Peruvian dictator (performing a coup with its own name, called Fujimorazo) in Peru which took up arms with Sendero Luminoso (The Shining Path), a Marxist group founded and led by the abysmal Abimael Guzmán, deserves a mentioning (and the conflict a book of its own). Atrocities were committed on both sides, and the people of Peru did not deserve a brutal communist guerilla takeover, but not the brutal repercussions done by the military either. Sendero Luminoso is still active, but now as an underground group considered a terrorist group. Fujimori died on 9/11 in 2024.

p.84 *puipuiga manatu,* teoría de la protección, protection theory in Maori and Spanish. It is a hypothesis gaining more and more evidence, that reefs can regain their growth starting from the bottom, working its way up, which means that we have more hope of coral-reefs reviving (even though on a larger scale, they're dying left, right and center). Also, how cool is that creation myth? I love Sverre Holmsen for bringing it into *Sjungande korall.*

p.88 Bengt Danielsson is another man whose work I love.

p.98 *fakaleiti, fa'afafine, akava'ine, moe aikane* and *māhū* are all different words to describe transgender-persons throughout the vast and deep Polynesian, Southern Pacific history.

p.101 *Stora Havet,* the Big Ocean, a Swedish pop-album classic released by Jakob Hellman in 1989. He sings:

Jag såg Stora Havet idag
och jag förstod hur stort det var

I saw the Big Ocean today
and I understood how big it was

See, I don't think he really did.

p.104 Yeah, my version of DOGE would look a bit different than the crude state takeover-one we got.

p.105 *Andelshamn* is a harbour in which you rent a space for your boat or ship, then collectively own the harbour. *Pro primo* means first of all. "Ere the red Sun rises!" is not a typo, but it is what Theodén shouts as the Riders of Rohan charge the enemy army at the battle of Pelennor Fields (in the movie version).

p.107 Ola Magnell is another great, down-to-earth, radical Swedish song-writer. Apparently, this song is dedicated to the Swedish organization Fältbiologerna (Nature and Youth Sweden).

Natten är här och alla katter är grå
men i den svartaste timmen, min vän
finns så mycket att lära, då är gryningen nära
då ska dagen snart randas igen

Tiden är sen och jag slår upp mina blå
mot hela rymden och vad ser jag i den?
jo, att allt indirekt i universum är släkt
vi är stoft av en stjärna, min vän

The night is here and all the cats are gray
but in the darkest hour, my friend
there is so much to learn, the dawn is near
the day will soon break again

The time is late and I open my blue (eyes)
up towards all of space, and what do I see?
well, that everything, indirectly, in the universe is related
we are stardust, my friend

p.108 *haggis* is a disgusting, slow-cooked, Scottish dish which
is basically Sheep's heart, liver and lungs wrapped in sheep
stomach. *kæstur hákarl* is a disgusting, slow-cooked Icelandic
dish which is basically rotten shark. True story. And this is
not merely the words of a vegan such as myself. It seems to
be the common view on the two dishes, especially the
Icelandic "delicacy", competing with the Swedish rotten
herring and a few other dishes as the world's most
disgusting tastes. There is even a display at a museum in
Malmö, Disgusting Food museum.

p.109-110 *otai* is a Tongan fruit drink made of water, coconut
milk and the flesh of fruit. *kava* is the Tongan and Marquesan
word for a mildly psychedelic drink made from the
perennial pepper-plant Piper methysticum, grown
throughout the South Pacific. *Umukai*, meaning 'food from
the oven', is the national dish of the Cook Islands. The meal
is cooked in an oven that has been dug out of the earth called
an *umu*.

p.113 The gods, the Valar, of Tolkien's world in which Lord
of the Rings takes place (Arda) is known for being able to
clothe themselves in the form they *choose and feel regardless of
gender* as they descended into the world. And all the trouble
in the world began when the macho-man Melkor (later

Morgoth) started to sing his own, disharmonic tunes in the choir-work that created the world.

p.114 *Benplockerska* was coined by the Swedish poet Katarina Frostenson when she took a fierce, harsh stance *against* the #metoo-movement in Sweden, after accusations (and later sentences) of her husband, Jean-Claude Arnault, "The Culture Profile", raping and groping women. She used it to describe the *women* in this case, called them *benplockerska* (bone pickeress) and Megaras, conjuring images of them feasting on dead corpses and whatnot. It was a whole thing. I reclaimed it in my follow-up to the Swedish version of Caribbean Wind, Polynesian Storm, (*Benplockerska* which was nominated for the queer award Prisma by Page 28) and used it for how radical people calling trans-women fake and claiming we have ulterior motives with transitioning makes you feel. Like a *benplockerska*. Come on, you guys. We don't need that. You're on the side of conservatives and fascists here. And as a transgender-person, you feel subhuman enough as it is.

riche nouveau means newly rich in French.

p.116 *satori*, Japanese, Zen-buddhist word for "enlightenment".

p.117 *hajj* is the holy Muslim duty of pilgrimage, *fata morgana* is "a complex form of superior mirage visible in a narrow band right above the horizon" named after an Italian translation of Morgan le Fay, a fairy-queen in the Arturian legend, *Kailash* is a holy mountain in Tibet, *the Damascus-light* was the epiphany by Saul which made him Paulus (deadnaming him much?) and convinced him to carry on spreading the teachings of one Jesus Christ, and the *Ariadne-thread* is a thread Ariadne used to get out of the Crete labyrinth where Minotaurus ruled in Greek mythology.

p.119 Yes, and the lovely World Wind is a concept I picked up from rappers. Black Moon, fronted by one of Brooklyn's finest, Buck Shot, in the song *This is What Is Sounds like (Worldwind)* draws on Asian, pentatonic rhythms (of one the best beats by Black Moon), makes it a vague-but-rising, seducing anthem of go-get-ism. But my interpretation of it is how Houman Sebghati mentions it in his dreamy *Världsvinden*, with the chorus of

Det var längesen, min vän
vi förenades i vinden

It was a long time ago, my friend
we united in the wind

That all of the winds in the world are one and the same, and unites us in our collective experience of them.

Epilogue

If you want, after reading this, want to

Reach out to and support the author:

Email her! preferably on arvidasvenskeauthor@gmail.com

Write to her on social media! for example follow Arvida
Svenske – poet, artist, journalist

https://www.facebook.com/profile.php?id=100092459993992
https://www.instagram.com/arvidasvenskeauthor/
https://bsky.app/profile/arvidasvenske.bsky.social

Visit her webpage!

Send her money so she can keep writing (and fighting)!

Change the injustices:

Read up on history, starting with:

Transgender history – Susan Stryker
Transgender Issue- an argument for justice – Shon Faye

https://blackculturalarchives.org/
https://www.blackhistorymonth.org.uk/
https://www.amphilsoc.org/library/CNAIR
https://sametinget.se/9688
https://pasefika.com/

Donate money to:

Organisations J-FLAG, ECADE, Cousins Cousines de Tahiti, GLAAD, all of ILGA.

Those that have less than you.

Act in a way:

that's not being homo, trans-, afro-, phobic, i.e. don't be a dick. Tell others to not be dicks. Vote. Organize. Decolonize. Write, scream and sing.

About the Author

Arvida Juni Svenske is a poet, a folk high-school teacher, writer and journalist born into this world as a woman, in a place called Stockholm, Sweden. Her names mean Eagle Wood June The Swedish One if you translate them directly, but why would you do that? She studied journalism in Stockholm, to be a teacher in Linköping and most of her twenties was spent in Malmö trying to find out who she was. Turns out she was a poet who in 2024 was about to publish her first comprehensive poetry collection in English, Caribbean Wind, Polynesian Storm published by She Rises. In it, she poured her heart as well as into processing the history of Sápmi-region in Northern Europe, the Caribbean, the Pacific Ocean Island as well as Central Asia, the colonial crimes committed there as well as the knowledge lost, especially other views on gender than the two-gender-norm being unsuccessfully carried out in most of the world. Arvida has released half a dozen poetry collections in Sweden and has written prose, journalistic and poetry in a number of magazines, both online and in print. She's currently writing a follow-up book that details her journey into womanhood, Estrogen speech.

LinkedIn:
https://www.linkedin.com/in/arvida-svenske-b5a14894/

Facebook:
https://www.facebook.com/profile.php?id=100092459993992